D1467140

finding

Mr. Rightstein

Copyright © 2016 Nancy Davidoff Kelton
All rights reserved
First Edition 2016
Published in the United States of America
Printed by Spencer Printing
978-0-9969726-2-8

Publisher's Cataloging-In-Publication Data
(Prepared by The Donohue Group, Inc.)

Names: Kelton, Nancy.
Title: Finding Mr. Rightstein / Nancy Davidoff Kelton.
Description: First edition. | Baltimore, MD : Passager Books, 2016.
Identifiers: ISBN 978-0-9969726-2-8
Subjects: LCSH: Kelton, Nancy. | Dating (Social customs)--Religious
    aspects--Judaism. | Mate selection--Religious aspects--Judaism. |
    Jewish men--Psychology. | Man-woman relationships--New York (State)--
    New York. | Single women--New York (State)--New York--Social life and
    customs. | Jewish wit and humor.
Classification: LCC HQ801 .K45 2016 | DDC 646.7/7--dc23

Passager Books is in residence in the Klein Family School of
Communications Design at the University of Baltimore.

Passager Books
1420 North Charles Street
Baltimore, Maryland 21201
www.passagerbooks.com

finding
Mr. Rightstein

Nancy Davidoff Kelton

Passager Books
Baltimore, MD
2016

for
Jonathan

Introduction

My father in his coffin looked better than most of the men I dated.

This speaks volumes about my father and the men. They ranged from okay guys to card-carrying loons who didn't have a nodding acquaintance with reality. Those in between were not quite single, not quite straight, definitely not monogamous, or not quite right. Not quite right included a Hebrew calligrapher. Two thousand years ago, he might have been a catch.

I thought I was missing the love gene. I spent much of my life missing Mom. She disappeared inside herself and then to hospitals when I was very young. "Cheer up your little Daddy," she said when I visited her at one.

Amusing Daddy took center stage. Soothing Grandma came next. She stayed with us when Mom was institutionalized even though no one invited her or wanted her around. One night I heard noises downstairs. My father was at a bridge tournament. My older sister, Susan, blasting her Platters record in her room, had a DO NOT DISTURB sign on her closed door. I ran down. In the breakfast nook, Grandma sat with her head in her hands. I put my arm around her.

"What's wrong with your mother?" she asked without looking up. "She has a cleaning woman, a husband who makes a good living, and everything to live for. What went wrong?" I had not even learned to write script.

"Mommy's going to get better, Grandma." I patted her head, feeling her thin white hair. It was sticky. Very sticky. I could barely remove my hand. "What did you put in here?"

"That spray in the bathroom. I wanted to smooth them down. How do they look?"

Grandma called her hair "they" and "them," not "it." She came from "the old country." English was not her first language. She did strange things with words. She called the ocean the "hocean." Cousin Eileen was "Hi-leen."

"Good, Grandma. *They* look good." I continued patting her head. I wanted to laugh. I wanted to cry. I wanted a grownup to hug me.

Instead, I added "jester" and "comforter" to my little-girl resume. Did these roles

a. provide basic training for my later life?

b. royally screw me up?

The correct answer is:

c. both of the above.

In my thirties when my marriage ended and my single mothering days began, I burst into tears one night over dinner with my friend Wendy. "I'm a little girl raising a little girl."

She put her hand on mine. "We're all little girls raising little girls." Even cool, collected Wendy lost it when it came to her kids.

Then there was dating. My journey, with men who proposed living together in holy matrimony or at my place and with those I endured for a meal or a drink, was not about putting Mr. Potato Head together. Along with mothering, daughtering, working, choosing, getting older, forgiving, and I hope, growing, it was about putting together me.

Like everyone, I am a bundle of contradictions. Comfortable one day. Terrified the next. Like everyone, I have demons, wounds, fears, and broken parts. Woven together with memories, moments, loves, and laughs they create a tapestry. A story.

This is mine.

Part One

In the Beginning

In the gray house in Buffalo in which I grew up, my mother didn't laugh or smile.

If she wasn't resting in her bed, she rested on the gray living room sofa and wheezed. If her asthma wasn't acting up, she paced. "I'm jumping out of my skin," she would announce.

When I closed my eyes at night, I pictured Mom jumping out of her skin.

One Sunday when I was seven, she took me to a piano concert at Kleinhans Music Hall to hear Van Cliburn. With his first chords, my mother smiled.

"The music's so pretty," she whispered.

All through the concert, I kept glancing at her. My mother's face was also pretty at Kleinhans Music Hall listening to Van.

"How about we go to a concert again next Sunday?" she said as we headed through the parking lot to Dad and our gray Buick. My father played chauffeur. Dr. Green, Mom's psychiatrist, said she shouldn't drive.

"Sure." *How about it?*

The following Sunday we saw Glenn Gould. He sat on a bench that was as low as our foot stool, did not have on a tuxedo, wore a wrinkled shirt, and had not combed his hair.

"He looks like an unmade bed," Mommy said.

No matter. Glenn's beautiful music made Mom look pretty again. "Nothing like hearing a famous pianist," she said as we clapped.

I cracked up. "It sounded like you said famous penis."

She laughed too. No one asked for my opinion, but I thought my mother would be happier, even cured, if she saw famous penises every week instead of Dr. Green.

I was eight when she was admitted to the Harding Institute, a psychiatric hospital in Worthington, Ohio. I called Harding "the nervous hospital." That made my gloomy father laugh.

A better-known mental institution, Menninger, in Topeka, Kansas, and Dr. Green's first choice for Mom, had no available rooms. I liked that. It meant that other people had mental patient relatives and that some were probably moms.

During my mother's stay, she talked to psychiatrists, had electroshock therapy and made necklaces with beads. My stomach ached when I pictured electricity in her brain. Still, I didn't miss her silence, her stern face, or her somersaults in the living room. I certainly didn't miss her chicken a la king.

Ever since I could remember, it seemed the only time she'd get near me was to set my hair. She would come at me with a plastic bag of bobby pins, sit me on the stairs and stick them in my head. "You don't want to look like an unmade bed," she often said.

Yes I did! Glenn Gould looked like an unmade bed. He had "gifts" that made Mom smile. Maybe I'd acquire gifts that would make her smile, too. And I liked being messy. Perfect-looking? No way. Not me.

The day I rushed home from first grade waving my first report card – all straight A's except in behavior – she stood at the kitchen counter with her back to me. "Shhh," she said. "I'm making Jell-O." She didn't turn around.

For my seventh birthday party, she insisted that the invitations not have the word "birthday."

"But it *is* my birthday," I said, choking up at the card store.

"It's not nice to make people think they should bring presents."

Of course they should bring presents. That was what birthday parties were for. I moved away from her to another aisle so her meanness wouldn't rub off. Her request was a first for the saleswoman; she had no other children's invitations. We went from store to store until Mom found a package of invitations without the word "birthday." I refused to speak.

That evening I ran away from home for an hour. The following day, I disappeared for two. My family thought I had run away again, and my mother called the police. They found me under my bed. My mother threatened to punish me by canceling the party. But my father said that would be too severe. Later, when my friends RSVP'ed, I reminded them I'd be turning seven and couldn't wait to open their gifts.

My sister, Susan, liked to say I "learned to deal with Mommy." No. I got around her. One night, before she went to the hospital, when she came at me with her bobby pin bag, I put an end to the pin curling by locking myself in the bathroom. "Little girls aren't supposed to look like ladies who go to Cecelia's salon," I told her.

"Everyone should have set hair," she said.

"That's for your opinion!" I called out, refusing to emerge until she put her bobby pins away. "That's for your opinion!" became my standard response.

Her illness turned me to my father, whose presence in my life grew. We played cards and perfected my Ping-pong game. "Nancy'll beat you left-handed," he'd tell my potential opponents, not mentioning I was a southpaw. At the ice-skating rink, no matter how cold it was, he stood at the rail, waving every time I came around. We oil-painted by numbers, took supplies from his office on weekends and went to Aunt Yetta's on Sunday afternoon for pinwheel cookies with pink and green food-colored swirls on top, and matching food-colored milk.

My first crush, the best-looking boy in the world, wrote poems. Walking home from school one afternoon before Mother's Day, he recited the following: *Dear Mom: We love you on Mother's Day and hate you on every other's day.* My crush turned into love. He spoke my truth in verse.

When tiny turtles came onto the scene, I got one. Not the first time I asked, but only after dragging my mother to the W. T. Grants pet department at the University Plaza whenever we did errands, pretending I wanted a parakeet. Mom didn't want extra living things in the house. She didn't really want those of us who weren't extra.

Eventually, she agreed on a turtle if I'd take care of it. I kept my Myrtle's bowl on the kitchen counter next to where Mom seasoned our food with paprika. I liked keeping everyone and everything close. I worried, though, that when my mother drank her highballs, she might pour paprika on my turtle.

I watched Myrtle sleep. Watched her climb rocks. Took her out and let her crawl on my hand. Spoke to her when I fed her in the morning and at night before going to bed.

Myrtle died the day the elephant at the Buffalo Zoo died. Dad took me there on weekends. Wherever we went, my father knew "the man." The food concession man told us the elephant would have a funeral.

I insisted Myrtle have one, too. I invited Grandma Cohen. She drove. Not well. Very slowly. She could barely see over the steering wheel. She didn't park well either. She parked her black Studebaker in the middle of the street.

On the Sunday afternoon after Myrtle died, Grandma, wearing a navy short-sleeved dress and a long, sad face, joined Susan, Daddy and me in the backyard. My sister had decided to wear her white blouse with her red and green plaid skirt. I wore my white blouse and plaid skirt, too. The four of us dug a hole by the backyard fence with the snow shovel. I glanced at the back door to see if my mother was on the way out. No.

"Shouldn't we wait for Mommy?" I asked.

Daddy shook his head. Dirt covered his cheek and forehead. I almost laughed.

I placed my dead little turtle in the ground in her bowl. Grandma, Susan, Daddy, and I covered it with dirt and then put tulips and dandelions on the mound. I kept checking the door and the kitchen window. No sign of my mother. She stayed upstairs the day we buried Myrtle.

I majored in bed-wetting. Bed-wetting brought Mom close to me. I needed her touch, her voice.

"Couldn't you get to the can?" she asked, changing my soaking wet pajamas and sheets the first time I summoned her in the middle of the night.

"I was sleeping." My Goosey-Gander lamp was off. She

couldn't see my face when I lied.

Her hair was rolled up in bobby pins. Before bed every night, she pinned it up after eating shredded wheat in the rocker by the TV. She wore a fancy, low cut, green silky nightgown with thin straps and lace trim around the crack between her breasts. Her bed head and bed body looked like they belonged to different people: a little old lady and Ava Gardner.

"You don't have to let this happen again," she said, tucking me in.

I made sure it happened again and again. While she got fresh sheets from the linen closet, I opened my bottom dresser drawer, and wanting her hands on me forever, I pulled out pajamas, not a nightgown, and a pair with buttons, not a slipover top.

"You can't keep wetting everything," she said.

I leaped up, and running my hand over my soaking wet bottom sheet that had been under me on my bed, I acted surprised. "Oh Mommy! Did I do that?"

Chuckling, she gently squeezed my shoulder. Yes! But she stopped rushing in so quickly and soon she stopped showing up.

To housebreak me, she replaced my cotton bottom sheets with a rubber one. I hated getting into bed. One night, I knocked on my sister's door and asked if I could come in.

"I'm sleeping," said wide-awake Susan.

"Please."

"Go away," she said. Her room was dark. I opened her

door a tiny bit, but couldn't see her face. If I turned on the light, she'd kill me. If I sat on her bed, she'd scream. I took a few steps, staring at the body under the blanket.

"Please let me come in."

"Why do you keep waking Mommy?" said the mound that was my sister.

"You know why." The darkness scared me. Susan scared me more. I stood at the edge of her bed, running my hand over the navy blanket she'd gotten for camp and wanted to break in. "I have accidents. If you let me stay, I promise not to talk."

Susan sat up. Her hair hung loose. She started wearing her hair in a ponytail a few months ago at the beginning of sixth grade. "You'll start laughing, won't you?"

"I promise not to." I crossed my fingers behind my back. "I won't even ask you to sing our song." At age six with Susan's help, I made up the words and melody to "The Davidoff Sister Song." It was my favorite song and it went like this:

> *We are the sisters, the Davidoff sisters,*
> *We'll never leave each other as long as we can stand it.*
> *My name is Susan (her solo)*
> *and my name is Nancy (mine)*
> *We'll never leave each other as long as we can stand it.*

She'd sing it once when I'd ask. We'd laugh. I wanted to sing it again and again. She wouldn't.

Except for having my mother's hands on me, the two

things that made me happiest were laughing with Susan and singing "The Davidoff Sister Song."

She looked over at me and said, "You're not really asleep when you tinkle in bed."

"I am too," I lied. "If you take me to the toilet, I won't wake Mommy."

She started to get out of bed. "Come on."

"I mean later. I don't have to go now," I said.

"I'm not getting up in the middle of the night." She lay back down and turned away. "Close the door when you leave."

"Susan, didn't you ever wet the bed?"

"Nancy, please. One baby in the family's enough." Her voice went out the window.

The next morning, I sat on the toilet lid watching my father shave as I often did. "I hate my rubber sheet."

Dad, in shortie pajama bottoms and nothing on top covering his dark, hairy chest, had shaving cream on half his face. "We'll get rid of it when you do your business in the can."

The can. At school, they called it 'the lavatory.' At home it was 'the can.' I looked outside. The tree between my swing set and the garage made shadows on the ceiling over the bathtub. The branches swayed like the arms and legs of a big monster. "I'm afraid to come in here alone."

My father puffed up his shaving cream white face. "Wake me. I'll take you, *tsatskeleh*."

He moved the razor down the side of his face.

How I loved that sound!

He rinsed his razor in the sink water and pulled the plug to let the water out. "We had an army phrase. 'Piss Call,'" he said. "Stand at my door and say Piss Call."

That night, I went to my parents' doorway. When I called out "Piss Call," my mother mumbled something and fell right back asleep. My father bounced up, led the way to the bathroom, and waited in the hall. "You only have to wash the hand you use to wipe," he said, walking me back to my room.

I did not ask if he was kidding. The nights he wandered down the hall and didn't watch me, I washed both hands. When he stood at the door, I washed one.

I needed my father. For Piss Call. For more.

The girls in the house did not like me.

Thank God for Daddy and for Geraldine, the cleaning lady. Geraldine was an incessant talker, smoker, and bra-strap adjuster. Not only were her bra straps never where they should be and falling on her arms, but she had buttons missing from her blue stained uniforms, which she fastened with safety pins. She moved upstairs and downstairs with a lit Camel in her mouth. Her ashes fell all over our rugs. She carried around a mop and detergents.

I don't remember seeing her use them. She coughed and talked to me.

She told me my mother gave her too much work. My mother complained, not to her face but to anyone who would listen, that Geraldine was a slob.

Although I already thought my mother was wrong about most things, I didn't say "that's for your opinion." I thought she might be right about Geraldine.

No matter. I adored her. I needed her. Unlike Mom and Susan, she did not shut me out. When we talked, we looked into each other's eyes. Had Geraldine been my classmate, she would have stood one ahead of me in the size-place girl's line.

"Are you related to Mary?" I asked one afternoon.

"Who's Mary?" Geraldine said.

"The lady who used to work here."

"Was Mary colored too?"

I nodded. Part of Scary Mary's job had been to feed me. She put a plate or bowl of food in front of me and shoveled it into my mouth without playing "open the tunnel" or other games. My mother would pass through the kitchen to check on us, or stand at the sink doing something else – anything else – saying, "Nancy's a good eater" or "Nancy won't give you trouble" or "Nancy'll pack it in." Terrified and obedient, I opened the tunnel and packed it in.

"You think we're all related?" Geraldine asked.

I did. The only black people I came across were women who worked for whites. "Not 'cuz of that." I sensed I hurt Geraldine's feelings. "Mary came by bus, too."

"Just 'cuz we're colored, ride buses, and clean houses, don't mean we're related." Geraldine headed upstairs.

I followed. "I'm sorry." Sorrier that Geraldine and other colored women had to clean white people's dirt.

Another day, after I learned that a second cousin killed himself, I ran down to the basement, bursting to tell Geraldine. She already knew.

"This world's too much for some folks." Coughing, she folded a towel.

I took the lit cigarette from her mouth.

"You can't smoke that, child. Your mama'll shoot me."

I put the cigarette under the faucet. "Smoking's bad for you." My father had just quit. "My mother wouldn't care if I smoked. She doesn't care about anything."

"Part of your mama's problems is that she sits around with nothin' to do."

My face got hot. "She does a lot, Geraldine. She shops and cooks dinner."

Geraldine looked into my eyes. "She doesn't have to lift a finger. That's how come she's unhappy. Your daddy spoils her. It's different from the way he spoils you."

I ran upstairs. Now Geraldine upset me. I could say and think what I wanted about my family and myself. An outsider could not. Geraldine saw and spoke the truth. Daddy spoiled me. He spoiled Mommy, too. And yes, she had problems. Problems too big to hide.

A short time later, Geraldine stopped showing up. She never called. She had not spoken of quitting, finding another job, or having had enough of me. No one fired her. That was what my father said. He thought she was sick, moved to warmer Alabama to live with her son and his family, which included three children, and did not want us, particularly me, to know.

A new cleaning woman came to work. She wore freshly pressed white uniforms and made our house sparkle, saying "Yes ma'am" to my mother and very little to me.

I missed Geraldine, the cleaning lady who didn't clean.

A few months before my mother went to Harding, she spent three weeks at Sisters' Hospital on Main Street, fifteen minutes from our house. One afternoon, Grandma Cohen picked me up from school wearing her gray Persian lamb coat and waited across the street where parents in cars lined up. In her black Studebaker, her head was barely visible over the steering wheel.

I pointed her out to my best friend, Sally, explaining I wouldn't be walking home with her. Seeing not much more than Grandma's white head cracked us both up.

"Where is she taking you?" Sally asked.

I hadn't told her about Mom. "To the hospital to visit my mother."

"What's the matter with her?" Sally said.

"She sick, but not sick like the flu or like the kind of disease people get in jungles."

The hospital parking lot was filled. Grandma drove round and round. A space opened up where a nun pulled out. I didn't know nuns drove.

In the lobby, crosses and Jesuses hung on the walls. They hung on the walls in my mother's room, too.

She had on new, bright aqua silk pajamas. Compared

to them, her face was pale. She seemed so far away. At her bed, I leaned over to kiss her. She kissed me, not smiling though, moving back to sit against her pillow creating a space between us. When I handed her a shoebox filled with brownies Grandma and I made, she put them unopened on the night table.

I picked up the box and handed it to her again. "Have one, Mommy. They're delicious."

"We used your recipe, Esther," Grandma said quietly, sitting on the chair by the window.

My mother took two bites of one, put it back, and passed the box to me. "Good," she said, still not smiling. "They're bringing me supper soon. I'll have more after."

I finished her brownie. Grandma shook her head when I offered her one.

My mother did not ask me about school or anything else. When a nurse appeared with a chart and took her pulse, she turned to her, smiling, and then told Grandma and me she was tired and we should leave.

"Cheer up your little Daddy," she said when I kissed her goodbye.

My father explained that Mom's psychiatrist hoped bed rest would cure her.

Her three-week "rest" made her worse. She came home sadder and angrier, wanting even less to do with me. I thought she did not get cured at Sisters' Hospital because nuns ran the place, disliked that she was Jewish and only helped Catholic patients, who crossed themselves.

Mom returned to lying on the sofa, sitting up in the afternoons to watch "The Kate Smith Show." She only spoke to me when I joined her before it started and we'd guess whether the neckline on Kate's dress would be scooped or high or V. I sat as close to her as I could get until the end of the show when Kate sang, "When the Moon Comes over the Mountain."

Like "The Kate Smith Show" and piano concerts performed by famous penises, Broadway musicals cheered my mother up.

When we saw *The Pajama Game* at the Erlanger Theater, my parents bought the cast album. I took it to Sally's house. We learned the songs. I suggested we perform the show for our families.

We rehearsed at her house every afternoon. Her freezer was filled with ice cream sandwiches and Sara Lee cakes, not packaged bread and Birds Eye vegetables like ours. Her mother, still wearing her skirt and matching monogrammed cardigan from her afternoon bridge game or lunch, insisted our snacks include fresh fruit. I insisted we eat the Sara Lee cake, frozen. The frosting tasted better cold.

The living room became our theater, the area by the fireplace our stage. The family portrait of a smiling Sally with her older brother, Richard, and their mother hung above their sofa where in my house hung an oil painting of a boat. They looked like a mother duck with ducklings, a captain with mates, announcing to the world they were stronger as a unit than alone.

"Do you mind being the man?" Sally asked one day after we sang Syd's and Babe's duet, "There Once Was a Woman."

"Fair is fair," I said. Sally won Rock, Paper, Scissors. A good thing, too. She was prettier. *That* I minded. *That* was unfair. Particularly when grownups rubbed it in. "Sally's precious" and "Sally's a doll," they would say with me standing next to little precious.

If I played Babe, the audience would laugh.

The good news: I got first dibs on the supporting roles. I picked Gladys. Her big number, "Steam Heat, "called for jazzy dancing and finger snapping. In one scene, Gladys gets drunk.

Not being the pretty one meant working harder, acting kooky and figuring things out. Sally had it easier, though. Pretty girls do.

A week before our big Friday night show, we handed everyone in our families homemade invitations. We needed costumes, including men's pajamas for the last scene when Syd wears the bottoms and Babe wears the top. Sally's father didn't own pajamas. Daddy did. One night, while reading in bed, he told me to take a pair from his dresser.

"Those will swim on you," he said, seeing what I chose. "Roll up the bottoms or you'll trip."

I had not asked my mother for the aqua silk Chinese

pajamas she wore at Sisters' Hospital. Those wouldn't work for Syd. And Mom hadn't worn them at home. Maybe she left them at the hospital. Maybe a nun was running around in them. Would God punish a nun for wearing aqua silk pajamas? Probably not if she obeyed him, kept on her headpiece, and did good works.

I learned not to ask her for much. Or talk to anyone in our family or out about Mom's illness. Like getting around being the pretty one, I figured some things out.

Friday after school, I went to Sally's. Her Grandma Lil and Great Aunt Bea came for dinner: lamb chops, mashed potatoes, and canned peas. When Sally's mother served homemade cherry pie, Richard excused himself. An argument started. I liked that Sally's family argued and wasn't perfect.

At seven-thirty, I called my house. The line was busy. I tried again. My sister answered.

"You're coming, aren't you?" I asked.

"To what?"

"*The Pajama Game.*" My stomach started to ache. "It's tonight. At Sally's." How come Mom and Dad didn't remind her? Did my play matter to them? "Her family's all here." My voice quivered.

"I forgot. I'm going to a party," Susan said.

I couldn't breathe. "Can't you go to your party after?"

"No," she said.

A little before eight, Richard reappeared with a girl in a red flannel poodle skirt and another couple. After our performance, they were going to their high school dance.

I stayed in the foyer on tiptoes looking out the front door window. Sally's mother tapped my wrist. "Look who's coming up the walk."

My father. Alone.

Daddy stepped inside, putting his hat, like the kind Frank Sinatra wore, in his hand. "It's nice and warm in here."

"Where's Mommy?" I asked.

My father's eyes went from Sally's mother to Sally, now beside me, to her father, on her other side, and finally to me. "She can't make it, honey."

Sally and her mother both put their arms around my shoulders.

From the living room, Richard called, "Girls, we're waiting."

Grandma Lil and Great Aunt Bea sat together on the couch.

"Come sit, Max." Sally's father ushered Dad to a comfortable chair.

Sally and I sang our songs and did our routines. As Syd, my knees shook. I could not look at Sally or belt out the words. But as Gladys, the stage became mine. I forgot the audience. Forgot my mother and sister were not there. My voice did not come from my throat, but from someplace further down. My hands and feet followed the music, taking on a life of their own.

After each number, everyone applauded. I looked around at our audience: at the eight people there for Sally. And the only one there for me. We got a standing ovation.

I took my final bow.

After school on Monday a little before four o'clock, I turned on the television and sat close to my mother on the sofa to guess about the neckline on Kate Smith's dress. Mom reminded me she wouldn't wear the same kind two days in row.

The game ended when my mother went to the nervous hospital. No one in my house watched Kate Smith or her necklines. The moon stopped coming over the mountain. It stayed behind it way too long.

Grandma Cohen moved in. She baked chocolate chip cookies with nuts. And shells. Whether she forgot to remove them or didn't see them, we had no clue, but Susan almost choked on one.

She boiled chicken, which turned out rubbery. The leftovers became rubbery chicken salad with too much mayonnaise.

Worse than her food was her long, sad face. Like the long dark dresses, she wore it all the time.

I couldn't get close to Grandma for the hugs I wanted. Or to anyone.

My father played games with me: gin rummy, casino, Ping-pong, Clue, hide and seek, and beauty parlor. At the hair salon I set up on the living room sofa and end table, he let me be the "beauty-tician" – my name for the hair-dresser – and style his balding brush cut into one of my two favorite hairdos: a bouffant or parfait. He laughed at how I said and saw things, at whatever I made up.

But he didn't hug me.

Laughing was Dad's way. It became mine. It helped.

It helped, too, that Daddy sent Grandma home.

"Ma, you'll come over on Sundays or we'll take you out for dinner, but the girls and I want to manage by ourselves," he told her.

Susan, Daddy, and I learned to cook (mostly burn) dinner. It turned out better when Aunt Yetta gave us step-by-step instructions on the phone.

Our weekend and evening shopping excursions to the A&P became fun. My father pushed me up and down the aisles in a cart and told strangers he forgot our grocery list, even though it wasn't true, and asked to borrow theirs.

At times, our house felt lighter, like a weight had been lifted. At other times, we limped around like a three-legged dog. By Sunday nights, our gray house felt grayer than it had when my mother was home.

At school, I got very quiet. In class, I did not raise my hand. One day my teacher, standing at the blackboard with her rubber tipped pointer, instructed us to open our arithmetic books to page 43.

I did not turn to page 43. I opened my yellow spiral notebook. Next, Miss Sullivan told the class to do the three long division problems on a clean sheet of paper. On a sheet of notebook paper, I drew three penises. They were not attached to men's bodies. Or to anything. On top, I wrote MY PENISES.

Oops! Penises couldn't be mine. I erased the "e" and

"s," leaving the word PENIS. In capital letters. After PENIS, I wrote SERIES. MY PENIS SERIES. I read and loved the entire *Bobbsey Twins* series. I could make my own series here.

Under the first penis, I printed V.C. for Van Cliburn, the first famous one I heard. Under the second, I printed G.G. for Glenn Gould. Miss Sullivan, now standing over me, grabbed my notebook.

"Go out to the hall!" The black rubber tip of her pointer was inches from my inkwell and even closer to my hand.

I smiled across the aisle at Wayne, who might have seen my drawings. My heart beat so fast I thought it would leap out and get to the hall before the rest of me. Miss Sullivan motioned me to the top of the stairwell.

"These are not your three long division problems, Nancy."

I had never been in trouble before or stood so close to a teacher. She towered over me. A good thing for me. When she spoke, she spit.

"They're not," I said.

Frowning, she glanced at them. "What on earth made you draw . . . ?"

I decided to help her along. "Penises," I said.

"You've never done anything like this. It's certainly not that long division is too hard for you."

"You're right, Miss Sullivan."

"Do you have an explanation?" she asked.

"The G.G. stands for Glenn Gould. The V.C. is for Van Cliburn."

Her face turned red.

I went on. "My mother took me to Kleinhans to see famous pianists. I thought she called them famous penises so I decided . . ."

"Never mind what you decided." Spit continued coming out of her red face. "Have you ever been benched?"

I shook my head. Being benched meant getting scolded by the principal and then sitting on the bench outside her office door. Everyone walking by – kindergarteners through eighth graders, their teachers, and the special education teachers who took kids out of the classroom to work with them alone – would see the poor benched, punished child.

"Miss Johnson is out sick." Miss Sullivan pointed her pointer to the corner where the two walls met. "Go sit there."

"On the floor?" I asked.

"Sit or stand." She started to go back inside. "If anything like this happens again, you will be benched. Is that clear?"

"It's not, Miss Sullivan." Being benched might be more fun than doing long division, which had nothing to do with life. Noth-thing. "You said if anything *like this* happens again. What is *like* drawing penises?"

Her face got as red as the brightest red Crayola. "You've never been a behavioral problem. I'm saying I'm letting this go. You're lucky Miss Johnson's out sick with the flu."

"Miss Sullivan, my mother's sick, too." I lowered my voice. "It's not the flu. She's mental. She's in an institution. She's staying there forever. She was in a Catholic hospital. We're Jewish so the nuns sent her home sick."

Miss Sullivan returned to the classroom. I sat outside in the hall on the cold, hard floor, listening to her go over the three arithmetic problems I had decided not to do.

Two days later, after dismissal my father came to school and squeezed himself into a desk with an inkwell in the second row. "You have to be younger and smaller to fit into these," he said to my teacher and me.

Holding a manila folder, Miss Sullivan pulled her desk chair over to him. "Thank you for coming in." She had sent a note home with me.

"Hey, it's for Nancy." Daddy winked at me. "Everything okay here?"

"Her school work is splendid, Mr. Davidoff. She grasps every subject except science. Her mind wanders during science." She turned to me. "Do you know why?"

"I don't understand science."

"I never understood science either." Dad glanced at me again in his we're-on-the-same-team way. "Nancy said you were upset."

Miss Sullivan took off her glasses. They were attached to a gold chain around her neck so they rested on her breasts. "Nancy mentioned that her mother's in an institution."

Daddy nodded, pursing his lips. "That's right."

"And that she's not coming home."

Daddy gulped. "That's not true." To me, "Why did you say that, honey?"

I shrugged. "We don't talk about when she'll be home."

Daddy looked at the inkwell. "She will be. Soon enough."

"That'll be wonderful for everyone." Miss Sullivan opened the folder and handed Dad MY PENIS SERIES. "Nancy started drawing these during arithmetic. Do you know what they are, Mr. Davidoff?"

Daddy seemed to be studying them. "I think so."

"Perhaps Nancy needs another outlet," she said.

"What kind of outlet?" I asked. "Drawing's fun."

Miss Sullivan went on. "Dr. Norman, our school psychologist, could speak to her."

"Dr. Norman?" I shook my head. "She gave our class a test. No one understood her. She talks like a ventriloquist." Dr. Norman also had a mole on her cheek. I didn't mention that. Instead I imitated the ventriloquist school psychologist by asking Daddy and Miss Sullivan if they watched "I Love Lucy" on Monday, trying not to move my lips. "How can I talk to somebody who can't talk?"

Dad smiled. I made him smile. Again. I was getting good at that. "Nancy has a point, Miss Sullivan. How 'bout she and I discuss this further at home?"

"Fine," Miss Sullivan said. Then to me, "Do you promise to stop drawing penises in school?"

"I promise." I almost giggled hearing my teacher say "penises." Instead, I put my hand over my mouth, turning my lips down to make a super serious expression like I did when Sally and I had straight-face contests.

Daddy. Thank goodness for Daddy. No matter what I did or said or drew, he was on my side.

I did not draw penises again. Or see the ventriloquist psychologist with the mole. My father and I did not "further discuss" my drawings. What a relief! A relief, too, that Miss Sullivan grabbed my notebook during long division before I initialed the third penis, the only penis I had ever seen.

It wasn't a famous one either.

The year after my mother's breakdown, she had a hysterectomy. I went around telling people, "We had Mommy spayed."

I wanted everyone to know she had a physical illness this time. I wanted to convince myself that she had regular problems the kind regular ladies had. Although she did not get all mental again, her distance, discomfort, and moodiness did not disappear, particularly it seemed around me. All through my adolescence, her lack of empathy and disparaging comments, particularly about my looks, hurt.

My nose was long. A ponytail accentuated my bad profile. My hair should be set at night so I'd have a style that framed my face. Unlike Susan and Daddy, who had natural smiles and photographed well, I did not. When we shopped for clothes for me, she'd tell the saleswomen, "She doesn't have much a neck." I thought that when they'd leave our dressing room they went looking, not for appropriate styles for me, but for parts of my missing neck.

When I asked her if she thought I was pretty, she said, "You have inner beauty." I sort of knew what she meant, but I wanted outer beauty. The kind boys noticed. The kind that excited Dad.

My kindred spirit father reinforced Mom when it came to my looks. Both, in awe of chiseled, blonde beauties, they'd remind me I was not one, not like Susan's friend, Ellen. "What do you say we nominate Ellen for Miss America?" Dad asked one day when he and I were playing cards.

"Gin," I said, laying down my winning hand. Like Mom, he made it clear I did not qualify for the crown.

Part Two

Eye Openers

My mother's life improved once I was out of the house. With Susan already on her own, she relaxed, happy to be alone with Dad, who loved being doted on. They took up golf. She was the better player. They rented an apartment in North Miami Beach and eventually bought a condominium in Pembroke Pines.

I was happier, too. Away at college, the face in the mirror belonged to me. I had new friends, mostly from or around New York. I fit in. I dated. I felt free.

By the time I graduated from college, I had acquired three useful tools:

1. Playing show tunes and standards on the piano;
2. Decisiveness; and
3. Acting happy when I was not.

I also acquired a husband. During the fall of my senior year in college when I told my mother I wanted to marry my boyfriend Don right after graduation, she suggested I wait at least a few years. Accustomed to pretending I knew better, I didn't listen.

Who, in her early twenties, admits that her parents know something? Anything? Besides it was the Sixties. Getting married after college was the thing to do. My sister, single and not about to tie the knot, got to be the different one. I not only thought I'd best conform; I feared ending up alone. I urged Don to propose. He did.

Not counting dormitory rooms, I went straight from my parents' house to my marital apartment without passing "Go."

I wanted love. I wanted a child. I wanted to be a better mother than mine.

Talk about being ill-prepared.

Playing house came easily. On my way home from my job teaching elementary school, I'd grocery shop and then cook casseroles, stews, fondues, teriyakis, and all kinds of veal and chicken dishes. Don and I threw dinner parties on weekends, went to friends', went to movies, plays and restaurants all over Manhattan, traveled, and had shares with other couples in Fire Island beach houses.

Living together was the surprise. Who knew at age twenty-two what a relationship was about? We moved through our days and nights with jobs, interests, friends, and evenings out, doing what I thought was expected, but we didn't have what Grandma Cohen called "great rappaport."

I could point a finger and blame my husband for what went wrong. It wasn't like that. Blame did not figure in. It takes two not to tango, two not to dance. We saw the world from different wavelengths.

I did not know how to ask for what I needed. Or even have a clue what that was. I'd want to talk. I was anxious. I obsessed. In my writing, obsessing worked. In my marriage it did not.

We became parents without being comfortable with each other. I was uncomfortable with myself. Mildred, my first therapist, pointed out that I looked to Don to fill the hole my mother had not filled.

He left on a Monday. A Monday evening in September.

In less than two hours, the Giants would be playing the Eagles in our living room in color. He left anyway. In a navy pinstripe suit.

As he walked out, I mentioned it was Monday. He asked if Monday was a lousy day to separate. I told him I meant that I couldn't believe he was walking out of our marriage on a Monday night in a navy pinstripe suit. He said he had no choice: the beige checked suit was at the cleaners.

Although I have blocked our parting words from my consciousness – the ending was too sad, too painful – I am positive we were not exchanging one-liners. We had not been doing well, but I never expected him to walk out that night or I would have broiled something less expensive for dinner than swordfish which was then $10.95 a pound.

"What you're telling me is you're not a team. You don't click," Mildred said weeks before.

Sometimes it seemed that simple. I knew it wasn't simple at all. The only thing I could say about what caused our demise: I was pretty sure it wasn't the swordfish.

As un-simple as marriage was, separating was painful. Hell. Thank God for my therapist and my unofficial therapists: my friends.

Louise called most mornings between seven-fifteen and seven-thirty. "Your wake-up call" or "Time to get cracking," she'd say. Or because we'd been friends since seventh grade and had been through everything together, she would be more direct with "Just making sure you're alive."

One morning, she suggested we go to the movies. "When are you free?"

"Every day and evening for the rest of my life."

Ordinary People was not the best choice. Who knew?

"That sure lifted my spirits," I said as Louise and I walked out of Cinema 1 onto Third Avenue on Saturday afternoon.

She put her arm around me. "Sorry. Mary Tyler Moore wasn't so perky."

I glanced up at my friend's long dark, freshly blown-out hair, then at her brown leather bomber jacket and nice-fitting jeans. "I liked Mary better with Lou and Rhoda." I liked perky me on those long-ago Saturday nights, too.

"I think the next movie we see should be *The Sound of Mucus*," I said.

The Sound of Mucus, my name for *The Sound of Music,* used to crack us up. I tried to smile, but tears streamed down my cheeks.

Louise took out a tissue from her Prada bag. "You didn't cry this much during *Funny Girl.*"

"Life was easier then," I said.

In the summer of 1968, we sobbed through *Funny Girl* at Buffalo's Granada Theater. Sitting in front of us, high school classmates, together since our junior prom and newly engaged, were making out. I didn't think "Lucky them." I thought "Lucky us."

The light changed. Louise gave me a peck. "We'll speak tomorrow."

I grabbed her arm. "Don't leave."

"C'mon up Monday afternoon. I'll ply you with liquor. It worked for me."

When Louise's first marriage ended, I invited her over and made a huge pitcher of Brandy Alexanders. I called my husband at work to tell him what happened and to please be sensitive to her. When he walked in, Louise and I were drunk on the living room floor, laughing.

She made divorce look like so much fun I decided to give it a try. If only that were true.

"Monday Emily has a play date. Then I'll be making our supper. We didn't have kids when you and Craig split up. Booze isn't what I need, anyway."

"What *do* you need?" she asked.

"Just let me cry," I said.

Moments later, as I beat myself up for my marriage's demise, Louise interrupted, "STOP! Stop blaming yourself! The problem was that he didn't get how special you are." It was the most loving comment a loving friend could make and exactly what I needed to hear. In high school, when Louise struggled with geometry, my father said, "Louise knows just enough math to get by, but she knows what's really important."

Yep!

In seventh grade, the first time I went to her house after school, her mother said, "Nancy, why don't you stay for dinner?" I stayed. I stayed all through high school. When we both moved to New York at age twenty, I stayed for dinner at her apartments whenever I could. Louise kept me on the American plan.

But now she had to leave. She and her husband had evening plans. "Nance, it's rough for you, I know. I promise you your time will come."

My father, a lawyer, specialized in estates. When he

spoke to his chronically ill client, Bessie, he'd ask, with a chuckle of course, "When Bessie? When?"

Irene, my college roommate, did not say my time would come as we sipped club sodas in the lobby of The Essex House where she and her husband, Elliot, were staying. We spent the afternoon at MOMA and now waited for Elliot to join us for dinner. After they got married, they moved to Portland and came to New York once a year.

Before I introduced them, 5'10" Irene had been self-conscious around boys. In high school, when a male classmate asked her if she would like to go to the senior prom, she said, "I would, but no one's invited me."

"That's what I am doing," said the boy.

"What would you do in my shoes?" I now asked her.

But Irene was not in my shoes. She had been advising me on how to be alone while we waited for her man.

She shrugged. "You're the one with the ideas. Put your sense of humor to use."

"How?"

"How should I know? I don't have one." Irene motioned our waiter for the check. She and Elliot treated in my town and theirs.

"True," I said.

Of course she did. The morning in September 1965, when we noticed each other in the restaurant of the Howard Johnson's Motor Lodge in Cleveland across from Western Reserve University, Irene and her mom were heading to a table. I sat with my parents in a booth. We had on almost identical outfits: navy shells with madras A-line skirts;

Irene's was taller. The other incoming freshmen stared at Ho Jo's floor. Irene and I, making eye contact, smiled.

"That one towering over her mother has a pretty face," my father commented.

Pretty. Inviting. Warm.

Later, when I saw her unpacking in a room down the hall in the dorm, I poked my head in and said I'd see her later, delighted we'd be living so close. That night, I arrived early in the lounge for the floor meeting. Most of the girls appeared in jeans or cutoffs. Irene shuffled in wearing pale pink man-tailored pajamas and furry bedroom slippers with her hair up in rollers emphasizing her long neck.

Motioning her to the seat I saved, the first words I uttered were, "You look like a giraffe."

Our laugh fest began.

As a college freshman, I dated boys in Zeta Beta Tau fraternity. Irene stayed in. If it bothered her, she didn't discuss it or complain, but she applied to NYU and transferred there in the middle of our sophomore year, commuting from Hewlett, Long Island. When I decided to attend NYU on a junior-year program, her father urged her to live with me in a dorm.

"Nancy's very sociable. You'll meet people." He didn't mean people. He meant a guy.

Irene and I roomed together. The first week of school, I met Don. A month later, at my suggestion, he brought his roommate to our dorm for dinner. Irene and I laughed the whole time. The following week, she and Elliot went out alone.

That was that.

And here we were: Irene, the giraffe, and little Miss Sociable me.

Life had a way of evening out. Which girl now had the Toni?

Two mornings very early, I was awakened by crank calls. The first time no one said anything. I thought Louise must have dialed my number and dropped the phone, or disappeared to wake her son or turn off her coffee. I said her name twice. Then I heard heavy breathing. The second time, a man whispered obscene questions about my erogenous zones. I called the police.

"Do you know any men who might not like you?" the policeman asked.

"My ex-husband, but he wouldn't make calls like that."

"Oh, so you're divorced?"

"Separated," I said.

The policeman asked more questions. "So you're separated and in your mid-thirties," he said. "Maybe I'll come over to finish this report."

The crank calls stopped. I did not meet the policeman; however, his acknowledging my new status as a single woman made me blush. A little flirting here and there might spice up my life again.

Except I had no room in my repertoire for flirting and spicing. I did most of my crying in therapy. During one session, Mildred, said, "Go treat yourself to something new. Something different."

Instead of taking the subway a block from her 66th Street office and going straight home, I walked to Bloomingdale's and bought a reversible down coat: khaki on one side, pink on the other. It was the most expensive down coat in the store and the most expensive article of clothing I ever bought for myself. I had wanted a down coat for ages. My mother and Don had told me down overpowered me. Until now, my coats were wool.

Wendy, my friend in the penthouse, a fashion designer, and my new notify-in-case-of-emergency person, had the last word on my clothes. "Stunning," she said that evening when I walked in wearing my new coat. "It's stunning on you." Wendy loved saying "stunning" if something hit her right. "The sleeves are perfect. The length, too." Opening her hall closet, she took out a black sheath. "Here. From my new line."

It fit great except for the length. It needed to be hemmed.

Before we became friends, Wendy and I used to see each other in our building lobby and at the pre-school our daughters attended. *She* was stunning. In her show-room, she modeled her designs for buyers. Like Louise and Irene, Wendy was tall, pretty, and married. I had no marital, height and beauty requirements for my best friends. It just worked out that way. I think.

Our first conversation occurred one day in the mail-room. She opened her new *Glamour*, and noticing my essay and byline, said she read my pieces in the last issue and the one before. "I've never known anyone in a magazine three months in a row who's not a fashion DON'T." Later that week, she called me from work. Her husband had to take out buyers that evening. She and her daughters were ordering in barbecued chicken and ribs. "C'mon up."

"What should I bring?" I asked.

"Emily," she said.

After eating, she gave me clothes from her latest line. "My husband does a lot of entertaining. Come up for dinner whenever you want."

I wanted. A few evenings during the week and sometimes on weekends too, we became a regular thing. An all-girl family.

Wendy liked eating at home after work. I liked going there. After dinner, she and I sat at her table, talking. About everything.

"You're the first good friend I've had since high school," she said one evening. "It's the first time I ever pursued anyone."

Wow! And she was so tall and chic. "It's the first time I didn't do the pursuing," I said.

Another evening, feeling particularly scared and overwhelmed as a single mother, I burst into tears.

"What is it?" Wendy said.

"I'm a little girl raising a little girl."

She put her hand on mine. "Hey, we're all little girls raising little girls whether a man comes home or not. What's harder than being a mother?"

Food, clothing, a place to hang out and let it hang out several nights a week. The bad part about being at Wendy's: getting in the elevator and going home.

The day after she gave me the black dress, I took it to my neighborhood tailor to be hemmed. He sat on the floor pinning it up. Since he opened his shop eight years before, I brought in whatever needed altering. As I stood on the stool in front of his full-length mirror, turning as he pinned, I mentioned I was separated.

"You should come in sometime without your dresses," he said.

My neighborhood tailor wasn't just pinning my new cute black one. The putz was now under it.

I walked out of his shop in my half-pinned black sheath and went to a tailor down the block.

I wore my new black dress, without the pins, to a New School faculty reception at the university president's 11th Street townhouse. After speaking with the few instructors I knew, I stood in my usual spot near the dining room entrance where the wait staff emerged from the kitchen carrying platters of food.

A bespectacled man with thin stringy hair, positioned in the same spot, started talking to me over the crabmeat canapés. His pants came almost up to his chest, indicating he had a very high waist or no clue where it was. He reminded me of the dorky boys at camp socials and bar mitzvahs, who asked me to dance while the cool guys asked the cool girls. Some things in life never change, including the kind of guys I attract.

Encouraged by Mildred and my unofficial therapists, Wendy, Louise, and Irene, to converse with everyone who did not look like a hardened criminal, I continued talking to him.

The high-waisted instructor, a CPA by day, taught accounting at night and had relatives in Buffalo, my hometown. We had two surefire topics: chicken wings and snow. He asked me to dinner.

On Friday evening at Monte's, an Italian restaurant on MacDougal Street, we exhausted the two surefire topics over the relish tray of carrots and celery on ice. Our classes got us halfway through dinner, but my love of teaching and his wanting to quit didn't help. My reason for accepting his dinner invitation was not because I expected to have fun, but to prove to Mildred, the girls, and myself that I could get out of the house.

When it became clear we had nothing more to talk about I said, "This is not personal, but the babysitter is taking the SATs tomorrow and asked me to come home early."

It *was* personal. Very personal. But he bought it.

After dinner, he also bought cranberries and apples at Jefferson Market.

"What do you use those for?" I asked.

"Chicken salad. It gives it a kick."

I bought apples and cranberries, too. I also bought a chicken. I boiled it the next day. And added the fruits.

Yum!

My dorky date showed me that everyone has something to teach us, and proved to me that I could grow and learn if I continued reaching out and wearing my invisible OPEN FOR BUSINESS sign.

Except I wasn't open for business. Reaching out often frightened me. Being alone frightened me more.

I kept a huge, sharp knife in my top night table drawer. A few years earlier, a man had followed a sitter from the subway to our apartment. He had not gotten inside, but who knew if the next one would?

I told penthouse Wendy and Louise uptown that I slept with a knife.

"Maybe you'll feel better if you come up here to sleep," Louise said. "You and Emily can have your own rooms."

"No, but thanks. We have our own rooms at home."

"Better idea. Call Craig." Louise gave me her first husband's phone number. "You two would probably hit it off."

"No way." Craig, an ACLU lawyer, wanted to change the world. Louise had wanted to change Craig. I probably dug him more than she had. His values, anyway.

"Go for it whenever you're ready," she said.

Ready? Ha! Is anyone on Planet Earth ever ready to date?

I was the first person in my family to end a marriage.

My parents, saddened and sympathetic, asked what they could do. What my mother did was get chest pains. She was admitted to Buffalo's Millard Fillmore Hospital.

After a stress test and an EKG, the doctors ruled out a heart attack. They decided she had angina and put her on nitroglycerin. She felt better, was discharged, and had a follow-up exam the next week.

"It wasn't angina after all," my father told me on the phone.

"It was me, right?"

"Looks that way." He laughed.

Parents and guilt and illnesses, oh my! Maybe Catholic girls learned guilt from the nuns, but Jewish girls were born with it and had it reinforced at home.

I laughed with my father. For two seconds. Guilt was funnier when dumped on someone else's child.

In the divorce lawyer's reception area, I perspired, something I rarely do. I bounced up to talk to the receptionist, to use the rest room, and to talk to the receptionist again.

When the lawyer appeared, I perspired even more. He didn't smile. His face lacked warmth. Nothing in our next hour together put me at ease. During our second consultation a week later, he spoke in the same gruff manner and then asked with a wink, "Any additional ways you'd like me to service you, honey?"

I stood up and grabbed my opened file. "No further questions, counselor."

I was out of there.

My next lawyer was not a pig. Or a divorce lawyer. I hired him anyway, becoming his only client who was not a co-op. I found him likeable. Sweet.

One morning, before a four-way meeting at Don's lawyer's office all the way downtown, my new lawyer, Joe, met me at the green market at Union Square. He had never been there and wanted to check it out. Wherever the farmers put out samples of apples, pears, or cheese, I did my usual thing: I helped myself. On occasion, I bought what I tasted. Today was not an occasion.

"I'm not worried about you," Joe said, watching me sample a slice of a Fuji apple after a slice of a Granny Smith. "You won't go hungry. You can fend for yourself."

In some ways and in the short run.

I learned that as a child. On Sundays my family often ate dinner at Laubes Old Spain on Main Street. One night after stuffing myself with roast beef and mashed potatoes, I left no room for even chocolate or banana cream pie. I told the waitress I would skip dessert.

"Skip dessert? You can't," Daddy said. "It's part of dinner. It comes with."

Years later I bought him a deck of cards. The veins in his forehead popped out. "Whoever heard of paying for cards?" He opened his desk drawer and pulled out two decks: one said United Airlines, the other First Bank of Buffalo. "They come with."

Had I learned nothing else from my father – oh, but I did – I knew to take whatever comes with.

In my twenties, at a smorgasbord dinner with Don

behind me in line, I put healthy portions of several foods on my plate. "You handle buffets like a pro," he said.

I took that to mean he thought I could make my own way and helped myself to life's goodies, not that I pigged out.

What I could not handle: watching my marriage dissolve into stacks of white papers with black formal words. Twenty minutes after sampling foods at the farmer's market, I sat in a conference room with three men in suits. I glanced around the table at my lawyer beside me and, across from us, at my husband's uptight lawyer, and at him. He was more appealing than the other two.

I looked down at the document in front of me, unable to take in air. I could not talk business. Talk about us. About ending our marriage.

"I'll read this at home," I said. "I can't do it now."

I wore my new black dress to a luncheon for an acquaintance who was getting married for the second time. Like when I read a great writer's work, I felt paralyzed and inspired. The bride had something I lacked, but if she could get there, couldn't I?

Seated next to me was an NYU program director with whom I spoke about teaching. "You sound like you love it," she said. "Would you like to teach a course for us?"

The following week after filling out work forms at NYU, I stopped at the student employment office to post a sign for a sitter. A likeable-looking girl was asking the information person about jobs.

"Excuse me," I said, "but have you had babysitting experience?"

She had. For three siblings, her neighbors' children in Minnesota, and for twins in New York.

I asked if she'd like to sit for the most terrific four-year-old in the world. Her eyes lit up. She did.

"Do you want to meet that terrific girl now?" I asked.

Within seconds of walking into our apartment, she and Emily were playing, talking and laughing. She became our sitter for the next six years.

Every so often, things come easily. Every so often, things turn out right.

"What do you have to lose?" Mildred asked at my next session when I brought up calling Louise's first husband.

"Nothing," I said.

She nodded. "It's a win-win situation, Nancy." A win-win situation, a favorite phrase of Mildred's and among her words of encouragement for moving forward despite ambivalence or fear. How did anyone make nerve-wracking calls, buy coats, or take any steps outside their comfort zones without the urging of a shrink?

I once asked a psychotherapist friend what constitutes a good psychotherapist. Three things, he said:

1. The ability to comment insightfully and buzz in the right words at the right moments, which involved empathy

and listening well;

2. Charisma;

3. A talent for pushing patients uphill, beyond where they were.

Mildred had all three.

After my session, I called Louise's first husband.

Craig, happy to hear my voice, sounded even happier to tell me he had gotten married. His second wife, also an ACLU lawyer, was terrific. Someone I should meet. Maybe we could have lunch.

Maybe not. "Let's make a plan soon," I said. I hung up and called Louise.

"Perfect! They'll change the world together," she said. "I can't believe he's married again."

"Why not? You are."

When they first got together, Louise and her second husband could not keep their hands off each other. After a few years, Louise claimed he become rigid, morose, and oh-so-stingy. Her husband did not tell me what adjectives Louise became, but they moved from room to room in their classic six on upper Fifth and from their apartment to their East Hampton house like preschoolers at parallel play.

She preferred discussing her first husband's second wife. "So just remember, Nance, there's a lid for every pot."

"Does that make me a pan?" I asked.

"You're not a pan," Louise said. "You just keep picking Marty Goodman."

Marty, my high school boyfriend, was sort of cute, but not exactly sharp. That he liked me more than I liked him made me feel in control. The night before I left for college, Marty said, "Date other guys. It'll be a feather in my cap."

I smiled. "If I go out with other guys, I won't be back with the feather."

The next morning, as my father and I loaded the car, I told him about the feather exchange. My father and I laughed about Marty Goodman, the feather, and about every guy after Marty I ever tried to love.

Seven months after my husband and I separated, I had dates with two different men.

Ben, a friend of a friend, had a nice-looking face and a nicer-looking camel cashmere coat. He took it off in the West Village Mexican restaurant where he decided we would eat. I couldn't tell whether he had a strange physique or very strange body language – one shoulder seemed higher than the other – but the way he moved and sat, he looked as if he was on a coat hanger.

He sniffled a lot and was more than a tad effeminate. And more than a tad eager to split the check when I asked how much I owed. As Tevye said in *Fiddler on the Roof,* "It's a new era, Golde." Dating was different nowadays. If I wanted a man to treat me, I'd best not offer my share.

"Did you like the food here?" I asked as we got up to leave.

"Not bad, but not the greatest. And you?"

"It was fair." I would not have suggested Mexican food. The dinner did not go down well. "This restaurant would not be a repeat." I felt the same way about Ben.

At my door, he pulled me close and put his lips on mine. It made me a little tingly. How weird that I enjoyed Ben's kiss, much less allowed it when the only thing that turned me on all evening was his camel cashmere coat.

The second man, Stuart, was the first psychotherapist I saw after hours. He had been an NYU classmate. We had taken Abnormal Psychology together. Stuart got an A. I got a B.

When I bumped into him on West 9th Street coming out of his office, his arm was in a cast. He had broken it, but claimed he felt no pain.

"I'm on Percodan and something else," he said, smiling a big one.

Probably many things else.

Before I personally knew or dated shrinks, I assumed they had the tools to live a balanced life. I also assumed, like playing tennis with a better player, by being in their company, I would get better faster. Maybe "cured."

Stuart invited me to a movie for the following Saturday night. I said yes. My friends would be with their husbands. My daughter would be at her dad's. Week after week, Mildred reminded me to stay open. Going on dates was a "win-win situation." What did I have to lose?

During the movie, Stuart made several trips to the men's room, each time returning with white powder under his nose. He wiped it constantly, making loud nostril noises.

I said nothing until we walked out. Then I asked, "Are you doing coke?"

"Uh huh." He smiled. "Good stuff, too. It's a different high combined with my pain killers, you know what I mean?"

I didn't. I nodded anyway. Stuart was a shrink.

He went on. "It's tricky getting it up the old nose with one working arm. Wanna try a line?"

I shook my head. "Could you walk me home?"

Psychotherapists acted sane during our fifty-minute hours, but might be coke snorters or loons when our time with them was up. Being in Stuart's company made me feel healthy. Well.

My life began to take order. Or at least it had a shape. I got regular magazine assignments, taught on Tuesday and Wednesday nights, and saw Mildred on Thursday. On weekends, I looked forward to two long distance calls: my father's at ten on Saturday morning, and Irene's from Portland between eight and nine on Sunday night. After Dad and I filled each other in, I would ask to talk to my mother.

"Nancy wants to speak to you," he'd tell her.

More often than not, I'd hear her say, "What about?"

I did not laugh. My father did. "What am I gonna do?" he said. "You know your mother."

"I do." Maybe not. Maybe I knew her like we all know our mothers. Not real well.

On Sunday nights, after Irene and I caught up, she would say something uplifting like: "You're fine the way you are" and, always, "Take care of Little Nancy."

Whenever I pictured the two of us, 5'10" Irene and

5'almost-2" me, in the late 1960s leaving our dorm, Rubin Hall, at 10th Street and Fifth Avenue to walk to class at Washington Square, or through the Village, or to Wo Hop in Chinatown on Sunday night for their special lo mein, I longed to be a college junior again.

At age twenty and a smoker, I regularly tried to quit, but then I'd go back to it when I crammed for exams. Because I was uncomfortable pestering the smokers on our floor for cigarettes, Irene did some of the pestering for me. A math major with little reading for her classes, she'd set her hair in huge rollers and get into bed much earlier than I did. I would keep her up, talking. She did not mind.

Little Nancy and the giraffe. Living with Irene had been a breeze.

Dad's and Irene's calls became the two things I counted on each weekend. No. I actually counted on four: their calls, loneliness between Saturday morning and Sunday night, and my mother's "What about?"

My neighbor, Diana, and I chatted in the evenings when we left our apartments at the same time for work. I would be carrying a folder with my students' manuscripts. Diana would be dressed in something flashy, often gold lamé.

Diana was a hooker. A high-class one with bleached blonde hair and a terrific body, who worked at home during the day and out of a hotel at night. The first time we spoke, Diana told me she was a cocktail waitress. The doormen told me differently.

Her regular weekday customers included: a short man with a big belly; a tall young guy with long hair who wore denim; and a significantly older white-haired tenant in our building. He and Diana had matching black poodles which they would walk together mid-afternoon.

Once Diana knew I knew what she did, she talked about her work. "I have no idea what you write about, but it can't be as interesting as what I come across," she said one evening. "Maybe you should interview me or follow me around."

"Maybe I should," I said. *Maybe I should.*

At the health club where we both belonged, she wore perfume and gold jewelry and had a beeper strapped to the waist of her tight, sexy workout clothes. I would see her having private conversations with the trainers, not about her abs. When I asked her why she didn't take funky aerobics, a popular, fun class, she said, "My clients' calls would bother everyone." Diana was the only member who used the club's phone for personal matters and frequently got paged.

One evening on our way to work, she asked why she hadn't seen my husband lately. I told her we were separated. She gave me a quick once-over. "You don't look ready to move on."

I was afraid to ask what she meant.

She invited me to a party at her apartment Saturday at eight.

It was between going and not sleeping. Diana frequently threw parties. I had not been invited to the previous ones, but the music and voices kept me awake. At eight-forty on Saturday, I rang her bell, wearing black slacks, a pink scooped-neck top, and a little more eye makeup than I did to class. Her décor was plain. The only furnishing that hinted at her line of work was a blue velvet canopy draping her bed.

The guests' outfits did, too. It was a toss-up which made me feel more out of place, not wearing a skin-tight jumpsuit or not being buddies with the pimps. The men had slicked-back hair, pinky rings, and huge cigars. They looked like friends of Nathan Detroit's. The women, in boas, sequins, and metallic outfits, left little to the imagination. It was *The Best Little Whorehouse in Texas* and *Guys and Dolls* without singing, talent, or a score.

After pointing me towards the bar, Diana left me to my own devices. I approached a man who looked different from the others, not exactly like an Exeter graduate, but not like a pimp. After responding to my comments about the stuffed mushrooms and the Latin music, he excused himself and moved on.

I knew how to converse with new people at most social functions, from the golf awards dinners at my erstwhile in-laws' Long Island country club to gatherings the Quakers held. At Diana's party, I could not connect with the dip. The only icebreaker I thought of was "How's tricks?" No one noticed when I left.

At home, I put on my Mike Nichols/Elaine May LP and listened to the telephone operator sketch, then the doctor and mother sketch. Talk about good company.

I got a legal pad. My pen started moving. I wrote a two-page sketch between an uptight woman and a weird guy on an uptown subway. She ignores him as he tries to pick her up. Then he mentions he's a surgeon. Her face and tone change. She invites him to meet her mother. I wrote another sketch between an actress and a whiny podiatrist on a first date, and a third between a woman and her male therapist.

When I looked at the clock it was three a.m. I did not hear Diana's guests or music anymore. The party down the hall had ended. Mine had begun. Saturday night need not be the most pathetic night of the week. When I didn't wallow in self-pity and got in touch with my true self, I did fine. We don't connect with everyone. We're not supposed to. My pen and paper gave me far more joy than a roomful of hookers and pimps.

The next day I called my actor friend, Zack, and read the sketches. "Let's perform one of them," I said. I already found out that Sunday was Newcomers Night at The Improvisation.

"Let's not, Nanceleh."

After several conversations, Zack said okay. For months, we worked together honing the material. We rehearsed the whole repertoire: the lousy first date, the doctor on the subway, and the patient with her therapist.

We decided we would perform the therapy sketch. Everyone in New York City was getting or giving therapy.

Everyone would relate.

The Sunday night of reckoning arrived. Twenty-one newcomers would be performing between twenty-one regulars. I was the only woman. How heady! Not only would I be fulfilling my longtime Dorothy Parker fantasy of being the funny lady at the table, but I would be blazing a trail for other female comics who had not ventured forth.

Zack and I were Number 12. Word got out that we were first-timers. As we waited to go on, newcomers and old timers gave us advice.

"It's all in the timing," said a fellow in a flowered shirt opened to his navel.

"It's more in the eye contact," said another guy who looked more like a fraternity pledge than a comedian.

"The audience will excite you. Just wait," someone else said.

I waited and I wondered. Why, with all their experience and wisdom, were these aspiring Dangerfields performing on newcomers' night and not warming up audiences in Las Vegas for Barry Manilow?

The guy in the opened flowered shirt had no timing. Or funny material. He got one laugh. I got a gin-and-tonic. The young one who claimed it was in the eye contact stared at his shoes when he performed. He didn't get any laughs. I gulped down my booze.

I heard the emcee call our names. Trailing behind Zack to the stage, I told myself the worst thing that could happen: we bomb.

Within seconds, the worst thing began happening.

Standing at a microphone, with bright lights glaring down at me and a sea of strange faces staring up at me challenging me to be funny, did not excite me. At first, nothing came out of my mouth. Then I whispered my lines. Neither the audience nor Zack could hear me. I did not make eye contact with him or with the audience, but only with the ring finger of my left hand on which I used to wear a wedding band and now had a bitten nail.

When we got off, Zack disappeared into the men's room. I found a table in the back and sat alone. The bartender appeared with a double scotch straight up and put it in front of me. "I thought you might need this."

I did. My hands shook. My knees knocked.

Zack reappeared, not exactly smiling. "What happened to you up there?"

I shrugged. New situations typically made my adrenalin flow. Not this one.

Zack took a sip of my drink. "We tried."

"We'll try again," I said. "Next week we'll do better. I already booked us."

"Nanceleh, tell me you're kidding."

"Let's talk tomorrow, Zack."

The following morning, I read my students' manuscripts. Then I finished writing an essay on becoming a single mother and jotted down notes on my career as a comedienne. The truth: I did not want to get out there and perform again at an hour when I would rather be home using dental floss.

I wanted to write and teach. Stand-up comedy was not

for me. I had ventured into a scary new arena, though. I could venture into others. Nothing is accomplished playing it safe.

NOTH-ING.

I didn't hear from Zack. I called him. "I was kidding about trying it again," I said.

"Bless you, darlin'." Zack told me he booked us for an ushering gig for Friday evening.

"Great! See ya, Friday," I said. "Good night, Gracie."

Heading to school one evening, I ran into Don crossing Fifth Avenue. I had gotten a haircut two days before. I typically hated my cuts, felt self-conscious about them, particularly right afterwards if the stylist blow-dried my hair, used mousse or gel, and gave me a beauty parlor look.

I had become more articulate about my hair with my beauty-ticians. Or at least what I didn't want. I actually liked my present cut. It framed my face. And as the stylist said, "It moves."

"You look nice," Don said, smiling. "I almost didn't recognize you."

"You mean 'cuz I didn't used to look nice?"

He chuckled. "Your hair looks good. It's different. Seeing you on the street is different, too."

Yes! And I saw the side of Don I had seen in my dorm cafeteria when he told me he loved me for the first time. He seemed so nervous. He turned so red. I felt his love for me. And mine for him.

As we continued standing on the corner in an awkward silence, what flashed through my mind was reading *Fear of Flying* in 1973. On my recommendation, he read it when I finished it. Then I lent it to my parents. My father called it a dirty book. My mother wondered what I saw in it. "Did you think this filthy book was so great?" she asked Don.

And he said, "Not as great as Nancy did, but I understand what it means to her as a woman and a writer."

He appreciated me in ways my parents couldn't. I appreciated that.

"I hear you did stand-up comedy," he said now.

"It was hardly funny."

"But you got up and did it."

"Yeah, but it was *really* hard." A lump formed in my throat. Marriage had challenged me. Ending one was the pits. Especially after being hit in the face with the realization that, in a different context and fuller light, the soon-to-be-ex was a good guy.

I took his wrist and looked at his watch. My class would be starting in three minutes. "I have to go."

This encounter had been harder.

Once a year, I saw my ob-gyn. He examined me, did a Pap smear, and wrote what he had to write on my chart without more than a "how are you, everything looks fine, see you next year." No chatting. No lingering. In and out.

Quick, quick, quick!

His waiting room was typically crowded. His second wife was the office manager. She sat at a desk ten feet from his examining rooms wearing a round-cut diamond ring the size of a car headlight.

In mid-divorce, I went for my checkup.

"Nothing appears different down here," said my ob-gyn on his stool, examining me, looking like he was about to stand.

"Nothing's doing down there. I've regained my virginity."

"How?" he asked.

"It's been a while. I'm separated from my husband."

"Oh!" He looked up at my face, remembering it seemed, after all these years, that I had one. "How do you like being on your own?" He continued sitting between my spread legs.

"It's different," I said. "I'm adjusting."

"I'd like to hear more, Nancy." This was also the first time in fifteen years that this man, who had been looking up me, called me by my name.

"Do you want to hear more about how it's different or how I'm adjusting?" I asked.

He didn't seem to hear me. Instead he tilted his head and in a low, seductive voice, said, "We should go have a drink sometime."

A drink? Sleazebags came in all shapes and sizes. They practiced law, tailored clothes, and did Pap smears on upper Park Avenue.

I sat up. My eyes went from my doctor's starched white

doctor coat to his leering smile.

"WE SHOULD NOT GO FOR A DRINK," I said, speaking louder than I ever spoke in stirrups.

And we didn't. I took my vagina to a female doctor.

Part Three

Love and Lust and Found and Lost

I met Robert at the East 72nd Street Playground in Central Park one Saturday after brunch at Louise's. I was pushing Emily on a tire swing. He was with two slightly older girls at the slide. We noticed each other at the same time. When Emily headed to the sandbox, I sat on a bench close by. He and I continued smiling. Our simultaneous smiles made me blush.

His body language conveyed an earthy sensuality. His faded cutoff jeans, torn tee shirt, and coarse features set him apart from the porcelain-looking Upper East Siders. I wondered if he had a wife and if he didn't how I should approach him.

I didn't have to. He was beside me within seconds.

"Are you sitting or pushing?" he asked.

"Resting."

He told me his name. I told him mine. We chatted. When he asked me for a date and I accepted, his adorable smile widened as if nothing could delight him more.

His daughters wondered who I was. He boldly announced, "Nancy, a new friend."

When my daughter asked the same, I whispered, "Robert. I'm not sure."

First encounters can be telling. From the start, Robert made it clear he wanted a commitment and some hope for a future. I was consistently ambivalent.

"I'd like to share my life with you," he said, after three months. "It's that simple."

Not for me. Despite interminable lonely nights and weekends before meeting him, I was not in a rush to finalize my divorce or plan a future. Not with Robert, anyway.

For one thing, our differences loomed large. I grew up in a home where everyone played instruments, loved the theater, and read. Robert grew up in a family that had little interest in the arts.

One night during a game of Charades with our kids,

he made the sign for book and held up two fingers. I called out *Moby Dick*. My daughter poked me. "Why'd you say that?"

I whispered, "He only knows one book."

It was *Moby Dick*.

But our cultural gap became window dressing. Much with Robert felt right. Divorced five years, he wanted to get married again. To me. Every day I woke up giddy.

And he was hot. He made me feel sexy. Womanly. Free.

"His sex appeal's his calling card," Louise said in her kitchen one evening when she had us over for dinner.

"Is it that noticeable?" I whispered, watching him leer from her dining room table. Was he leering at her?

"Christ, he oozes it. He knows how to use it, too."

Right.

I ignored – or tried to ignore – *that*. And what could be a more troubling problem. Robert said that when his marriage went south, he strayed. Cheating, for me, would be a no no. I told him so. Then I let it go.

After all, he and I were happy. New. Why would Robert cheat?

Besides, no other men were in hot pursuit. Robert was into me.

During our first year, I had moments – glorious moments – when I actually put my ambivalence and fears aside. Maybe we could build a life together. Maybe Robert was "the one."

I thought so on my birthday. After an afternoon of tennis, he gave me chocolates, champagne, and a Ray

Charles album wrapped in *The New York Times* with one red rose on top, because "this is how I see you," he said. We had a romantic dinner and danced in my living room to "Georgia on My Mind" and "Ruby."

I thought so on weekend outings with our kids; at movies, on bike rides, and in each other's apartments, when I would play beauty parlor with the girls, and then we'd cook or go out. The girls' squabbling in the back seat over who sits at the window and who gets the middle with the hump irritated me. On the surface. On Saturdays and Sundays, the five of us often became a family. A Brady-ish bunch.

One morning while walking through Washington Square with Robert, we ran into a family of four I knew from the playground, each parent holding a child's hand.

"They're such a happy family," I said, staring longingly.

"You're a happy family, too. You and Emily," Robert said. "And when you include me, and me with my kids, we're all a happy family."

We were. For a year and a half. Then Robert started issuing ultimatums. And other things cropped up.

Like ending my marriage for real. My husband and I reached an agreement. Our divorce papers were ready to be signed. Signing would mean an official ending. A death in black and white.

Endings. Departures. How did people move along?

I could not sign my papers. Or build a life with a new man. If Robert and I were to tie the knot, what would happen in three or seven or fifteen years when our passion waned? When only one of us would be reading?

I needed to go slowly. I had said "I do" once. I meant it. Maybe my marriage should not end.

Don's phone call one evening after eleven confused me even more. "I was made partner today," he said.

"Wow!" A lump formed in my throat. "Congratulations. Your mother must be calling everyone in the world."

"I'm calling you first."

First! Still first! My throat lump got thicker. How did people handle these things?

Damned if I knew.

At a diner one morning having a bagel and coffee, I took a multiple-choice stress test in *The New York Times.* A middle-aged woman with a gray bun sitting close by, seeing me circle answers with a pencil and thinking I was circling ads for jobs, asked if I was looking for work.

Hoping that teaching and freelance writing would cover my expenses, I had not sought out other work, but it had become increasingly difficult to make ends meet. I told her I was.

The woman, a bookkeeper at an employment agency specializing in the arts, said her boss, Elizabeth, needed someone to make calls. She handed me a business card. Ten minutes later, I called Elizabeth from a pay phone outside the restaurant, set up an interview for the following week and went to Bloomingdale's where I bought a plain beige cotton interview suit.

That evening I wore it to Wendy's. "It's nicely tailored," she said. She rolled up the jacket sleeves and held up the skirt to show me the length my new tailor should make it. Walking around me, she went on, "You can wear that anywhere."

"Where will I wear this after the job interview?"

Wendy shrugged. "To your next one."

"How come you didn't say the suit is stunning?"

"I like it and you look fine in it," she said. "It's just not exactly you."

Not exactly.

"Is Robert exactly me?" I asked.

She shrugged again. "I dunno."

"What do you think?"

"It looks that way. You're happier than I've ever seen you."

"You've only been seeing me for five years. That's how long we've been friends."

"So don't give me the job of deciding if Robert's right for you."

On her hall table was the notice about the possibility of our building being converted into a co-op. I had gotten it the day before, too. "Will you buy your apartment if this happens?" I asked. As insiders, we would get a good deal.

"I think so." Wendy and her husband, also a fashion designer, had big salaries. "And you?"

"I don't know." I didn't know if I could afford my apartment, if I would get the agency job, or if I wanted it. I didn't know if I should sign my divorce papers, go back with my husband, or stay with Robert.

I knew I would not return the beige suit. I knew, too, it wasn't me.

Elizabeth Carlson, the owner of Carlson Arts Employment Agency, had on beige suit similar to mine. It helped. "Sit down, sit down," she said, pointing to the chair across the desk. "Looks like we have the same taste."

I nodded. "This suit can take us anywhere." My mother used that expression in praise of a classic dress or sweater. "It can take you anywhere." I have never spoken that way about clothing before. And this suit would not 'take me anywhere' other than here.

Tall and thin with patrician features, Elizabeth looked poised; however, smiling did not come easy and her eyes darted around the room. The two photos on the windowsill – one of her on a horse, and the other of her in a sailboat with an Ivy-League-ish-looking older man, both in evening clothes and displaying big, white teeth – would make one think nothing was hard for her anywhere.

She explained that she and her two reps placed graphic artists in all kinds of positions. She did the top-level place-ments. "I need someone part-time to make cold sales calls." She talked while she ate an egg salad sandwich, displaying a mouthful of white-yellow food. "Is that up your alley?"

I had never made a sales call. Hot or cold. I knew nothing about graphic arts.

In *Funny Girl,* when Barbra Streisand as Fanny Brice auditions for the Ziegfeld Follies, she is asked, "Can you skate?" With confidence she answers, "Can I skate!" She lands the job. In the next scene, she is klutzing around the stage in her skates, not in sync with the others.

Focusing on Elizabeth's egg salad, I answered a resounding, "Right up my alley. Yes."

She was out of the office my first day. On the second, she hovered. After overhearing several calls, she came charging in. "You don't understand the graphic arts. You keep calling mechanicals 'mechanics.' We don't place mechanics. You're very chatty, though. You keep people on the phone. That's great. That's great." She asked me to open up a publishing area. I would find jobs at textbook publishers, colleges, and corporations and get the writers, editors, and managers to fill them. "I'll give you a company credit card so you can take clients to lunch."

Lunch. *That* was right up my alley. "Sounds great," I said.

I sat between my parents in the eighth row center for a matinee of *La Cage aux Folles*. Whenever the three of us went to the theater, I sat between them, as I did with Irene and Elliot.

I had seen the show shortly after it opened and I hoped my parents would like it. "You're gonna love it," I said, my eyes lingering on my father, concerned that he more than Mom would squirm seeing homosexuals in love and singing drag queens.

Leafing through his Playbill, Dad asked, "Is it as good

as *The Miracle Worker*?"

Years before, after seeing *The Miracle Worker* in New York with my mother, Dad wanted to take me. A month later, we flew to the city one Saturday, watched Patty Duke and Anne Bancroft weave magic, and flew home that night.

"Different," I said.

My mother stood up. "I'm going to the can."

Alone with my father, I brought up my sister. She and her husband had bought a weekend house in Massachusetts and my parents were headed there from New York. I had not been invited or even told about the house until the closing. I had no clue this whole last year that she'd been house-hunting.

"How come Susan doesn't share things with me?" I asked Dad as I often had before.

"She can't," he said.

Can't? Or won't?

Whether "can't" meant a lack of ability or skill, or avoiding an uncomfortable place, "can't" to my mind was an excuse. A cover. A cop out. A way to get off the hook. Had Susan learned "can't" from Mom?

Can't or won't? I just didn't know.

The house lights dimmed. My mother, back from the restroom, apologized to the people in our packed row who stood as she passed them to get to her seat beside me. The orchestra began the overture and my father and I sat back. My mother did not. She poked Dad on the shoulder. In a loud voice so that he, the people around us and in the mezzanine could hear, she said, "Max, I need a hearing device. I won't be able to enjoy the show without one."

Neither would the rest of us.

Whether she really needed a device or had decided to be a pain in the neck I could not tell, but I knew it was my job, not my father's, to climb over the people in our row and possibly step on their toes to get what Mom wanted.

I did. I helped her insert it, too. She claimed it didn't fit. I wanted to shove the damn thing in. Finally, during the opening number, we got it in. She stopped talking, but continued to fidget. Did she know she fidgeted? Did she know how annoying her constant fidgeting could be? If I told her to stop, would I make her feel bad?

Life was so damn messy. The lines between the adult and the child were not clearly drawn. The good news at the theater that day: I detached from my mother and got into the show.

So did Dad. The story, acting, and Jerry Herman's score captivated him. When George Hearn as Abel sang "I Am What I Am," his eyes filled up with tears. "That was some show," he said, rising for the standing ovation, drying his eyes.

His tears did not surprise me. I had seen them before. Each June, when I boarded the Camp Tamakwa bus at the Peace Bridge, he waved good-bye at the window and let the tears fall.

He cried hard in 1964 when the doctor called to tell him that Grandma Davidoff died. The first time he cried in my presence was a decade before that, on a Saturday morning at Howard Johnson's over sunny-side up eggs. I was seven and we had just dropped my mother off at her psychiatrist's for her weekly appointment.

"What's the matter with Mommy?" I asked, taking the yellow of one of his eggs and giving him both my whites as we did at home.

"She's got problems."

"What kind of problems?"

"Up here." Daddy pointed to his head.

"What does she do at Dr. Green's?"

"They talk."

"What do they talk about?"

"I don't know, honey." His voice quivered. Tears streamed down his cheeks. He couldn't eat his one yoke. Or any of the whites. He could not have been any sadder. Daddy always ate everything that 'came with.'

Not long after that, during a Passover Seder at Aunt Yetta's when my mother was at the nervous hospital, the phone rang after I, the youngest of the cousins, finished asking the first of the four questions: "Why is this night different from all other nights?"

Aunt Yetta picked up the phone in her kitchen. "For you, Max. It's Esther." Mom never asked to speak to Susan or to me.

Daddy took it in a back bedroom and returned ten minutes later blowing his nose and wiping his red eyes. We finished the meal but closed our Haggadahs. I didn't ask the three other questions.

The night became too different from all other nights. My father sat there and cried.

Whether my mother shed tears for anyone or anything, I did not know. I never saw her cry.

On Saturday after *La Cage aux Folles,* Robert joined us at the Carnegie Deli, but because my parents were staying with me, he went home from there. Upon returning to my building, Dad headed down to the garage for the pills and sweater Mom left in the car. She and I were alone in my apartment.

"I can see what you like about Robert," she said, sitting next to me on the sofa.

"You do?" That surprised me. And it didn't.

She nodded. "He's manly."

"Very." I smiled. "I'm not planning on marrying him, Mom."

"I can see that, too."

What did she mean? "You do?"

"Sure. You're not divorced. You're learning about yourself. And what Robert has to offer. He's manly." Mom looked at me, smiling. "He goes for you."

"Right." Her understanding of people, of me, and of sex, or maybe of sex appeal touched me. My whole life I saw Dad and her as good parent/bad parent. It made my ideas of them simpler. Easier. Easier to pretend that he was tuned in and Mom was out to lunch. I moved closer to her.

"You think I'll get married again?" I asked, looking right into her eyes and she into mine.

"How do I know? That's for you to decide. I'd say you will." She went on. "When you *are* ready to get married again, make sure that thing – the glue, the romantic piece

— is there. Relationships are hard enough. That glue helps."

"Do you have that with Daddy?"

She blushed. "Can't you tell?"

Our first conversation about sex when I was twelve took place after a mother-daughter night at school that included a movie on how babies were made. When we got home, she went to her bedroom to sew. I followed her, firing away questions.

She told me to wait until I got married before "going all the way."

"But what if I fall for a garage mechanic?"

"Your probably won't, but if you do, it would be okay."

"To sleep with him before we're married?"

"No. Just sleep with him," she said.

My father, back with her sweater and pills, picked up the deck of cards still on the dining room table from our pre-theater casino and gin games. He turned to me. "What does that guy do again?"

"Robert?" I said.

"Yeah, Robert."

"He works for the city, Dad."

"A civil service job, huh?" He motioned me over to the table.

"Max, why do you care what Robert does?" my mother asked. That Robert did not practice law or medicine would matter to her, too, if he were to become my husband.

My father dealt out our gin hands. "Is he a forever guy?"

I picked up my cards. "I'm not sure what forever is, anymore. Right now, I'm just having fun." My face felt warm. Damn it! Did I really have to explain?

Dad wasn't done. "You'll fall for any guy who's interested in you, won't you?"

Nothing came out of my mouth. My face now felt as if it was burning. Couldn't he understand that men might find me attractive? And I might be attracted to men? Didn't he know his comments hurt? Was my being sexual more than he could handle? Or was it my desiring a man who was not him?

My mother went over to him and poked his arm. "Max, why don't you keep your big mouth shut?" She laughed, but sounded serious. "Nancy's a big girl. She does fine on her own. She doesn't need your permission or approval."

No?

I put down my cards without looking at my hand. "I don't want to play." This was the first time in my life I said that. The first time I didn't play his game. I headed to my room. Why hadn't I been more direct just now? Ever?

My mother started to follow me. "Nancy, Daddy didn't mean anything." She went back into the living room.

I closed my bedroom door. I heard Mom speaking Yiddish. That usually evoked laughter. It didn't now.

Wow! My father had no trouble understanding that I felt pushed away by my sister. He understood *La Cage aux Folles*. My mother could not get out of herself at the matinee. She understood me now.

Nothing and no one were all one way. Not in families. Not within ourselves. A bunch of contradictions. Wasn't that what we all were?

I signed my divorce papers. Without much fanfare. Or discussion with my friends and father. How unlike me!

I had been discussing it with Mildred every week, and twice a week when terror and anxiety flooded me, going back and forth. Back and forth. She heard me better than anyone ever had.

"I understand how difficult it's been for you, and that you don't feel one way," she said. "Let me put it like this: Does your gut tell you to stay married?"

"No."

That was that.

Not exactly. Robert had been waiting. Asking if I signed my papers. I had to tell him.

"Wonderful," he said, the evening I shared the news. We were at my apartment. Just the two of us, eating meat loaf I made with creamed spinach and baked potatoes. He opened a bottle of champagne he had brought a few weeks earlier, saying we'd save it for this occasion. "Now we can get married."

I gulped.

The Saturday before, I had found a lipstick in his medicine chest that didn't belong to me. He told me it belonged to a woman named Kathy, whom he recently started to see. He said he didn't love her. He loved me. He'd stop seeing Kathy if I would make a commitment.

I couldn't. History repeats itself. Leopards don't change their spots. I couldn't commit to a cheater. Or to a forever deal.

Timing. Timing. Timing. I had just untied a long-term knot. No way could I tie another. That night, instead of raising glasses of champagne, Robert decided we needed a breather.

The following afternoon I had an emergency session with Mildred. "Do you want to marry Robert?" she asked.

"No."

"Robert wants to get married, Nancy."

"But I just got divorced."

"So?"

"What about what I want?" I said.

"What about it?" Mildred asked.

"He could wait this out, couldn't he?"

She stared at me. "He's been waiting it out. Are you going to have a different answer?"

"C'mon. Admit he's lucky," I said. "I'm not making demands."

Mildred stared at me some more. I hated when she did that.

I went on. "He's getting the milk for free, Mildred. He doesn't have to buy the cow."

"Robert wants the cow, Nancy."

"What should I do?" I asked.

"Feel it. Learn from it. Then move on," she said.

I felt it, all right. I sure as heck tried to learn. Move on, though? What a pisser again!

On the bulletin board over my desk, I tacked up a sign that said: DON'T CALL ROBERT.

I called Robert. A lot. Sometimes I cried and couldn't

stop. Sometimes I cried a little.

"It's hard to get used to something and lose it," he said, sounding sweet and sympathetic during one of my jags.

His voice comforted me, but he didn't say he missed me. Or offer to come over.

I didn't ask about other women. I didn't want to know.

Without therapy, without a Mildred, Robert moved on. He had the power now.

I thought a visit to my West Coast friends would get me out of my funk. Irene and Elliot, in Portland, told me I could stay as long as I wished. I'd have the whole top floor at their new vacation house in Black Butte.

Nick, my Fire Island landlord and friend several summers before, now lived in St. Helena, and just finished building a guest house next to the pool. He would be happy to put me up.

So would Randy, a regular movie date in high school and now a screenwriter in LA.

I started in West Hollywood at Randy's. We schmoozed in his yard by his pool, swam, sat around and talked some more about our lives, Buffalo cronies, and work.

We had fun together. At first.

Towards evening, I overheard him on the phone. "This girl from high school's staying here. Who needs it?" He laughed. "No, I didn't invite her. She invited herself. Some guy dumped her and she's a mess." He spoke quietly.

Laughter punctuated his next sentences. Then I heard, "I'd love to see you. Let me try to figure this out."

I figured it out for him. I left early the next morning, two days early, for St. Helena. The first day Nick and I took a tour of a winery and had a blast tasting all kinds of reds and whites. At night, we swam in his pool and I slept in the new guesthouse. The second day while he went to his job, building and painting houses for a contractor, I wrote and swam some more.

That night he strongly suggested I stay in his room. With him.

Back east, I never got a whiff of testosterone from Nick. Or thought of him romantically. He once mentioned his last relationship had been in his twenties and it ended after a few months. His history, Peter Pan demeanor, and dirty clothes and fingernails pointed towards one big No Trespassing sign.

"It's not personal," I said, "but I'm trying to get over someone. I don't jump into bed just like that, anyway. And sleeping with you would ruin our friendship."

Then it occurred to me: Nick and I didn't really have a friendship. He had been my landlord one summer. I did not know him. I didn't know Randy either. Twenty-some years ago in high school, we went to the movies every few weekends. Since then, we'd had dinner once a year in New York.

I stared at the ceiling of Nick's guesthouse the second night, afraid to use the pool or the bathroom, afraid to move, unable to sleep. What if he did something strange?

There are no free accommodations, no free pools. Had I been utterly clueless to travel across the country to visit men with whom I wasn't close? Men I didn't *really* know?

I flew to Portland three days early. For two nights, I stayed with Irene and Elliot in their new big house that looked like Tara. Then we drove two hours and stayed at their Black Butte vacation home. Still holding hands, sitting close together, and kissing each other, Irene and Elliot did not act like love birds to make me jealous. I was, though. I had been the matchmaker. If I hadn't introduced them, they wouldn't be all over each other right now making me feel like Pitiful Pearl.

Fish and houseguests may smell after three days, but staying with men who are not romantic partners and happily married couples stinks. Irene may have been one of my closest friends, but staying in the top floor room of her weekend house made me homesick.

Homesickness. Was homesickness about being far from home or being far from oneself?

My father liked to say: we take ourselves with us wherever we go. I first heard it as a child. Dad sold his share of a lucrative family company to start from scratch on his own as a lawyer. Running a business gave him an ulcer. So did working with Uncle Abe. My mother asked if it bothered him that he was barely eking out a living while Abe was becoming wealthy. "No," Dad said. "I have to take myself with me."

I felt anxious we might be poor, but pleased with Dad's independence and courage to do what he wished. When

Abe returned from China and was discussing his next vacation to France, Mom said he was lucky to be traveling so fancy. Dad said, "The only problem with Abe's vacations is that Abe is taking himself."

The problem with my West Coast trip had little to do with my hosts. The problem with my West Coast trip: I had taken my depressed, unconscious self.

I couldn't wait to get home. I wasn't sure why.

After I unpacked, I stared at my DON'T CALL ROBERT sign. And called him. Several times. Each time we spoke, he was alone. Or said he was.

"Are you reconsidering?" he asked.

"No." I still wanted Robert to be my boyfriend. He still wanted me to be his wife.

Nothing changed. Nothing would. I stopped calling.

A play called *Shirley Valentine* with Pauline Collins opened on Broadway. I took myself – the self that loved the theater – to see it. It was about a sheltered woman's life before and after a transforming holiday in Greece.

Robert had been my transforming holiday. Like with that recipe I had gotten from my first post-marital date – Chicken Salad a la Dork – I added ingredients. Seasoned my life.

What a swell party we had!

One Saturday on our walk around Washington Square, Wendy said what she'd said several times before. "Most women would have married Robert."

"I wasn't ready. I'm still not ready. Besides, when the going gets tough, Robert cheats."

"Big deal," Wendy said.

I went on. "Regular cheating destroys trust."

Wendy didn't say anything.

I looked up at my friend with her long, easy strides, moving around our first lap as she did through life, with a nonchalance that eluded me. As close as we were, we did not delve into each other's psyches or relationships. No one understood the inner workings of another couple. And sometimes, the couple did not understand the deal they made for themselves.

I wished I could be in denial. I wished I weren't a confronter. I could see how denial and being tall and pretty spelled BLISS.

Part Four

Moving Along

The tenants received the letter. It became official. Our apartment building would be converted into a co-op.

"Lucky us," said Wendy.

"Lucky you," I said. For insiders with money, buying a piece of New York real estate – a two-bedroom apartment, yet – was a heck of a good deal.

In 1977 and four-months pregnant, I'd fallen in love with my present apartment upon setting foot inside. The alcove between the living room and kitchen would be my writing space. A room of my own. I could put a table in the kitchen for breakfast and lunch.

Perfect for family. Perfect for me.

Now I was a single mother with a seven-year-old daughter in a building going co-op, with no idea what to do.

Like most women who had grown up in the 60's, I was raised to buy sofas, ottomans and end tables: things that went *into* the apartment, not the actual apartment. I was a writer, instructor and part-time employment agent, not an orthopedist. I did what any normal woman with limited means and no experience buying real estate would do as she was about to receive a red herring: I panicked.

"What's a red herring?" I asked my lawyer, picturing a little bald man in a big white apron appearing at my door with a fish.

My lawyer said it was the preliminary offer. It arrived. So did the black book, the final offer, which looked like the red herring.

Next came Celia, a resident down the hall, who looked like neither. Celia, our self-appointed floor captain, appeared in my living room as many evenings a week as Dan Rather. On a nightly basis, she'd ask, "If the building goes co-op, do you know what you want to do?"

I did. I wanted to make Celia disappear and turn into the Prince.

Memos, newsletters, updates, and updates of the updates appeared at my door as regularly as our floor captain. Tenants who'd spent years ignoring each other huddled in hallways discussing their options. Two arguments in favor of buying: 1. We would have equity; 2. As insiders, we'd get terrific bargains.

Of course I'd buy. One thing I'd been raised to have, in addition to a teaching degree I could fall back on and a husband I could count on, was equity. And a bargain was a bargain. I hadn't found many in New York other than the Staten Island Ferry.

I listened to the two arguments against buying: 1. The monthly maintenance and mortgage payments would be substantially more than our current rent. 2. We could no longer just call the super and handymen for repairs.

How could I buy? My monthly income fluctuated from bad to very bad. My toolbox contained two items: a screwdriver and a hammer. Like my parents, I was inept with both. When anything needed fixing, they would "call the man."

The tenants formed four committees. The steering committee organized the other three. The engineering committee discussed plumbing and wiring. The communications committee wrote the memos. The legal committee did everything else. I joined the legal committee.

On three Mondays, I paid a babysitter $3.50 an hour so I could sit in another apartment listening to our evening's agenda and arguments about issues not on our agenda. I opened my mouth three times each week: to ask if I could call my sitter, to ask if I could use the bathroom, and to second the motion to adjourn.

I called my lawyer. "What should I do about my apartment?"

"Discuss it with your accountant," he said.

I called my accountant. "Talk it over with your father," he suggested.

I called my father, who asked, "What do your accountant and lawyer think?"

I agonized with my seven most intimate friends, including two on another coast, with cabdrivers I knew for seventeen city blocks, and with a couple sitting behind me at a Broadway show. The women all asked: Could I afford it? Wouldn't it be risky? The men I consulted all said I should buy it. How could I not take the plunge?

I quieted down to hear my voice. I heard: pro-equity. I believed owning beat renting. I believed, too, that I'd remarry within a few years, move into "his" more spacious apartment, and make a hefty profit "flipping" mine.

Most important, despite my terror, I wanted to take the leap. Robert Browning wrote, "A man's reach should exceed his grasp." What about a woman's? The leaps I'd taken – getting divorced and becoming a single mother, performing stand-up comedy, and refusing Robert's marriage proposal – had challenged me, and from each I grew.

"Congratulations," my father said when I told him I'd be buying. "Where are you getting your mortgage?"

Mortgage? I learned that mortgages came in different shapes and sizes with fixed and adjustable rates, and caps, ceilings, and points. I learned that nothing I learned about mortgages mattered. With my income, I wouldn't qualify.

My father co-signed my loan application. When he offered to help with the down payment, I said I'd manage. I wanted to prove to him and to myself I could take care of business on my own.

At the pre-closing, I read a stack of documents on which I saw numbers, huge amounts of money I must come up with month after month for thirty years. As I picked up my pen, my hand shook. I shut my eyes, and signed what needed to be signed. Then came the closing. I had a new partner: the bank.

Joan, a neighbor with whom I sat on the legal committee, asked if I wanted to meet a great-looking, divorced man who belonged to her temple. He headed their soup kitchen.

Sure. The temple. Their soup kitchen. Aunt Yetta would be thrilled.

I met Larry at Knickerbocker Bar and Grill on University Place at seven p.m. Already seated, he pointed to the hearing aid in his left ear. "Look directly at me when you speak," he said, "and make sure you enunciate." When I opened the menu, he reached over and closed it. "We'll order a glass of wine. Or coffee," he said. "I ate dinner at home."

I had eaten nothing since a yogurt for lunch. My stomach growled.

I ordered a merlot and smiled. Trained by a mother to show an interest in others — even if the others were slimy-looking and cheap (how did Joan get 'great?') — I asked Larry about his grown children and heard details about their jobs, food preferences, food allergies, experiences at summer camp, in college, and after. His daughter loved spending her wealthy husband's money. Larry asked nothing — nothing — about Emily. Or me.

He explained what he did as a financial planner and handed me a business card, then a bunch. "You won't need my services, but you can spread the word among your friends."

I put his cards in my pocketbook. "If I leave this very minute, I can get started." I did not say: *I can start spreading.* No double-entendres for Larry. It might give him fuel and make me puke.

"You have a sense of humor," he said.

"I'm not kidding, though. So what makes you say I wouldn't need your financial services?"

"Your income. Joan told me you're some kind of teacher and writer."

"Some kind," I said.

There are no free lunches, no free merlots. Will Mildred applaud or scold me when I tell her about my ridiculously polite behavior with this arrogant, cheap jerk?

"You're a funny gal. Joan didn't tell me you're funny."

"Joan wouldn't know." Then not to get heavy or mean because, after all, Joan might know other swell, easy-to-like guys whom I could date, I added, "She and I aren't close.

We don't socialize and all we've ever talked about is our co-op conversion."

"I've never seen Joan's and Ed's apartment."

"We have the same layout." I wanted to say: *You'll never see mine either.* Instead I stood up. "I'm actually going to see my layout now."

"Now?"

"I have a sandwich waiting. I'll get home on my own." I enunciated both sentences.

"Don't be ridiculous," said Larry. "A gentleman always walks a lady to the door."

I did not argue. I did not talk on the walk home. Had I spoken, it wouldn't have mattered. Larry couldn't hear.

In front of my building forty minutes after my allotted merlot, Larry grabbed me and gave me a French kiss, sticking his entire tongue in my mouth. I pushed "the gentleman" away and dashed inside.

Ten minutes later he phoned. "I just wanted you know I got home safely," he said.

"I want you to know I don't care."

I ran into Larry in the A&P checkout line a few months after almost gagging on his tongue. He couldn't quite place me. "You look familiar. How do we know each other?" he asked. His hearing aid wasn't in his ear.

In an extremely loud voice, so he, everyone in line, in every aisle, and I hoped in every store on Sixth Avenue could hear, I said, "At the end of a really awful date, you rammed your tongue down my throat."

❖

At the Carlton Agency I located jobs in textbook writing and editing and found capable applicants to fill them. Something different came my way: a request from the personnel director of a New Jersey college, a big graphics client of Elizabeth's, for a Director of Communications. The job required an experienced person to oversee a staff and all the school's communication.

I placed an ad and got an enormous response. Among the first applicants was a middle-aged New Jersey woman who, years earlier, had worked at a university writing press releases, memos to the faculty, and some of the chancellor's speeches. On staff for a year, but not at the helm, she left to become a homemaker.

She had seven children. Some were married. Two had children. Some were still in school, most were gainfully employed. All spoke to each other and to her and her husband.

Intrigued, I fired away questions about the children's early years. Sometimes two to four were in diapers and slept in cribs in the same room. The older children helped with the little ones. The family regularly sat down together for dinner. Everyone ate the same home-cooked meal: stew, ham, turkey, or meat loaves with several sides. The kids had chores, spoke their minds, and had differences of opinion, but as Ms. Mom put it, "Family's family. They figured out how to get along."

I arranged an interview for her at the college for the

following day.

Elizabeth, insisting I keep my door open, walked into my office when the woman left.

"How many other candidates are you sending?"

"None yet," I said.

"That's ridiculous. Ridiculous. That's not how we do business. I've gotten the college dozens of people for layouts and catalogues. They'll never use us again. Number 1: You're supposed to send as many people as you can for each job. Number 2: That woman hasn't worked in the real world or held a top position."

"That woman raised seven children. Quite well, it seems. I'd say she could do anything."

The following day after her interview, Ms. Mom called me. "I got the job," she said. "I start in two weeks."

Elizabeth appeared at my door eating an egg salad sandwich, talking with a mouthful. The head of the graphics department at the college had phoned her with a bunch of new top-level positions he wanted her to fill. He hoped she'd send people as good as the new communications director. He heard she was a gem.

"Very good, very good," Elizabeth said. "If you're interested in adding on more days a week, we should talk."

"Thank you. I'll let you know." I wanted to write. I wanted to teach. Two office days were fine.

There are different ways to skin a cat, my mother liked to say. At work, anyway, I got it. Elizabeth got it, too. She stopped hovering, let me keep my door closed, and reminded me regularly to take clients out.

The Oyster Bar became my regular haunt. For the three years I worked at the Carlton Agency, in between seeing Elizabeth's white-yellow mushed up food and listening to her say things twice, I did a lot of placements and had a lot of lunch.

If there were different ways to skin a cat at work, there must be different ways to meet men.

Behind my closed door, in between placing job ads, I placed a personal ad in *New York Magazine* and answered those that sounded promising.

My first date told me over dinner he did not "practice monogamy" and would never be a one-woman guy. I said I appreciated his upfront honesty, but that wouldn't work for me.

On the phone one night, another man, much younger than I, hearing Emily ask me for something, said, "Who's saying 'Mommy'?"

"My daughter."

He hung up.

An excellent conversation with a Columbia University English literature professor made me feel smart and led to dinner. And to another. And to a third. At the end of date three, we were still discussing *Jude the Obscure*. He didn't try to kiss me or even reach for my hand. I had no desire to get close to him either. Going slowly was my way, but without sparks, why bother?

I reached out to an older man, Hank, from Westchester who had two children with whom he was close, a steady job, only one ex-wife, many interests, and a love of Manhattan. Terrific!

"How about I take you to The Gotham for dinner?" he said.

Hank's thick graying hair, sweet smile, and ease talking when I met him at The Gotham turned me on. Conversation flowed. For eleven minutes.

Then he said, "There's something you need to know."

I didn't think so. All I *needed* to know before our entrees arrived was whether we were clicking and might consider a second date.

Hank went on. "I had prostate cancer. After surgery, I had radiation and chemo."

"I'm so sorry." I was, too. When my students write about their cancers, I find it hard to comment on their work. I'd rather give them hugs. When friends report that they or their partners or siblings or children have just been diagnosed, I listen and offer help.

"That's not what you need to know," Hank said. "I'm fine." He laughed a little *heh, heh, heh.* "Better than fine if you get my drift."

I got Hank's drift. I couldn't even manage a *heh.*

He continued. "I have a device down there so *when* we become intimate, there's something you'll be doing."

Oy!

Typically, on dates I asked tons of questions to bring the man out. I wanted Hank to go in. Shoving a warm raisin roll in my mouth, I put up my hand. "TMI, Hank. Too much information."

Over my miso marinated black cod and his soft shell crabs, I moved the conversation to fish: halibut, jumbo shrimp, baby shrimp, and salmon fillets. Next I went to movies, then to wines. The best I could do this evening: get this fine meal down.

The second I walked into my apartment, I called Louise. "I'm finished dating. Don't ask about tonight."

"Okay. Just tell me what you ate," Louise said.

"I had cod. My date had soft shell crabs and prostate cancer. Now he has a stent on his balls."

"Oh God, Nance! You saw it?"

"Of course not, but what do you think a device down there looks like?"

"Like the bicycle pump at the Hertel Avenue gas station we used for our flat tires," Louise said. "Picture a tiny hand pump. You'd have to pump it up and down, up and down, until you blow up his tire."

"I'm done with guys," I told Louise.

Two days later, I told my new therapist – Dr. Sigmund, I'll call him – the same thing. "I can't keep singing for my supper," I said.

Dr. S's tiny office smelled from whatever he ate for lunch. At this session, it was tandoori chicken.

"We sing for our suppers in different ways in all our relationships, Nancy."

He had a point. He also had dyed orange-ish hair that

didn't quite cover his gray, and a legal pad on his lap on which he took notes.

Dr. Sigmund, my second therapist since Mildred substantially raised her fee, was significantly older than the first, a very young free one at the counseling center of the college where I teach. She would excuse herself at least once a session after I'd say something that gave her pause, claiming she had to use the restroom.

But the restroom was to the left of her office, and she would turn right. A few minutes later, she'd return with a response.

I mentioned I had written four biographies for children, one on Harriet Tubman. She asked if I'd bring it in for her to read. She would give it back the following week. When I didn't see it at my next session, I asked where it was.

"I lent it to my mother," she said. "She's doing research on the Underground Railroad."

"You didn't tell her I was your patient, did you?"

"I've got to use the restroom. I'll be right back." She walked out, turned right, and returned a few minutes later. "Of course not," she said.

I terminated with the young, free therapist and her supervisor, whom she consulted when she turned right, and started with Dr. Sigmund and his legal pads.

I also started seeing a new man – Mitch – whom I met through the personals. He wore a thick gold chain around his neck. He became my boyfriend anyway. The chain wasn't the problem.

His clothes came from Lord & Taylor. The rest of him

came from the Bronx. His books came from nowhere. He had none. His apartment looked like Best Buy with multiple televisions in two rooms.

Mitch's coarseness, bad-boy good looks, and maybe even the chain turned me on. Did all women secretly dig rough guys?

"What do you and Mitch talk about?" asked Dr. Sigmund.

"Where he should park his car," I said.

Instead of nodding, responding, smiling the tiniest smile, or even glancing at me, Dr. Sigmund looked down at his yellow legal pad, noting what I said. His weekly note taking bothered me. I told him so more than once. More than once, he made a note of that.

One time he said, "I'm going to take notes whether you like it or not. This is how I do therapy."

During another session, he told me, "A big issue of yours is not accepting other people. I've become one of the people. That's transference. Now we can work on it."

Still another time when I said, "I feel you see me more as a case than a person," Dr. Sigmund's response was, "Whether I write on yellow legal pads or not, you *are* a case." Pointing to two piles of twenty-six to thirty legal pads on the floor, he added, "Those are my other cases."

Mitch, whom I'd been seeing for as long as I had been in therapy with Dr. Sigmund, while rough around the edges, was rougher at the core. Physically abusive to women before me, he was only verbally abusive to me. Not knowing his history initially, I assumed as I had with men before him, with everyone actually, that I, not the other person, was to blame. So Mitch's nastiness became my fault.

Dr. Sigmund reinforced the idea that intolerance was My Issue, something I needed to work on if I wanted a relationship. "You'll have to stop cowering and learn to handle and accept all of Mitch," he said.

"Even his rage?"

Dr. Sigmund nodded. Of course he nodded.

I got a whiff of Mitch's anger even before I met him, during our first phone conversation, which began with his giving me the details of his company's health plan – I hadn't asked about it – then went right into his pension plan and to his homeowner's insurance policy without inquiring if I had such things or an interest in hearing about them. On and on he went.

After keeping my mouth shut and politely uh huh-ing him for oh so long, I asked, "Are you reading a script?"

A pause. A long pause. Then he lashed out. "No, I'm not reading a script and that's rude of you to ask." Another pause. The anger filling the silence was palpable. In a very nasty tone, he said, "You obviously don't know how to talk and haven't been anywhere. You don't give people a chance." Louder now, he said, "I think we should hang up, but first I'm gonna give you some advice, young lady." I could practically see him wagging his pointer finger. "The next time you open your mouth to someone, don't ask if he's reading a script."

"I'm sorry." Not sure if I was truly sorry and wondering why I didn't let my gut guide me when I felt his anger through the phone wires, I apologized for being wrong and told him he was right. Maybe his accusation and tone scared me. Was my intolerance the reason I was alone?

The first time Mitch lashed out in person was after the first night I stayed at his apartment. We typically stayed at my apartment, but had attended an event near his so, at the last minute, we decided his was easier. On Sunday morning his doorbell rang at eight-thirty a.m. He was in the bathroom. I was still in bed. He asked me to answer it.

"Who'd be ringing your bell at this hour?" I didn't have a robe. Or any other clothes except the dress I'd worn the night before.

"Stan," he called out. Stan, his cousin, lived in the building. "I told you that before I started seeing you, he'd go get us doughnuts. We watch *CBS Sunday Morning* together."

"How did he know we stayed here last night?"

"I called him earlier when I woke up." Mitch emerged from the bathroom in his pajama bottoms, called to Stan he'd be a second, and handed me a flannel shirt. "Here. You can put this on."

It covered my backside, but wasn't much longer. "Mitch, I'm really uncomfortable. Do you think you might have asked me if it was okay to let Stan bring doughnuts?"

"This is my routine when I'm home." His eyes had daggers.

"You're with me, though." My voice quivered. "I'm not only a little vulnerable here. I assumed you'd want to spend the morning with me."

"Stan's waiting. I'm letting him in."

"Do you have a robe I can wear?"

He got a navy flannel one from his closet. "I'm not gonna talk about this anymore. If you'd rather get into your dress, I'll drive you home and come back."

I put on my dress, a semi-perky face, ate one doughnut, making small talk, and quietly asked Mitch to drive me home. We didn't talk in the car. The look in his eyes frightened me.

So did being alone.

He'd get nasty when I'd want contact or behave in ways to which he wasn't accustomed. After seeing movies, he'd cut me off when I tried discussing them. "Stop. Just stop, already. Most people would be deciding whether they'd get Chinese food or pizza by now. Enough," he said, walking ahead.

I told him his nastiness upset me. At my urging, he consulted one anger management specialist and then another. Nothing seemed to work.

I hung in and hung on for a year and a half. After he lashed out at me at a friend's party, I bid adieu to my outer borough beau. A week later, I bid adieu to Dr. Sig.

"Patients don't just leave," he said, too surprised to take notes. "There's a winding down. A whole terminating process. We can discuss how that'll go."

I shook my head. "I've wound down on my own. I'm terminating today. My time is up."

Marriage had been hard. Dating was worse. Meeting

men through ads was the pits. It all took too much out of me. And too much of my soul.

At least I knew a great therapist when I had one. I returned to Mildred the following week.

A few Halloweens, Emily and I marched in the Village Parade with Wendy and her daughters, all in costumes and part of the happening.

Most Halloweens, Emily got invited to parties and went trick-or-treating. One year, a classmate, with whom she had plans, came down with the flu at the last minute. Emily, already wearing my red lipstick, eye make-up, earrings and blue-flowered knee-length dress – a long one on her – grabbed her trick-or-treat bag.

"Bye," she said, heading down the hall.

I called after her. "Want company?"

Already ringing a neighbor's bell, she turned to me. "When I'm done on our floor, you can ride up with me if you promise you'll let me go by myself to people's apartments and wait at the elevator door."

I could. And did. At home later, we threw out the unwrapped candy and ate some of the rest. Emily, saying nothing about trick-or-treating alone, put a lot of the wrapped pieces in the orange and black bag we bought for her friend. "This should make her feel better," she said. "Right?"

I nodded. Right.

My spirits soared each Halloween. Then came the other holidays. T.S. Eliot had it wrong about April being the cruelest month. And Mother Teresa had it right: loneliness was the worst affliction. From early November through the New Year, I cried at Wendy's, in bed at night, and with Mildred.

My first Thanksgiving separated, Emily had gone to the Macy's Parade with her dad. It was freezing. After I bundled her up in her pink snowsuit and they left, I set the dining room table. A divorced friend and her son would be coming for dinner. I opened my fridge and looked at the two Cornish hens I bought. Two stupid little hens. I called Mildred at home.

"It's your first Thanksgiving as a single mother," she said. "It'll get easier."

It didn't. One Thanksgiving when Emily was with her father and I had no place to go and no person with whom to share it, I called my parents and said I would like to come down to Florida.

My mother said no. My sister and brother-in-law would be there. Having us all would be too strenuous for her.

"I'll be alone, Mom. If you don't have room, I'll stay in a motel."

She did not relent. She told me not to come.

"What kind of mother tells her child *not* to come for Thanksgiving?" Irene asked during our next Sunday night call.

"Mine," I said.

"What kind of mother tells her child not to come for Thanksgiving?" I asked Mildred at my next session.

"Yours," she said. "It's sad. That's who she is. She's not going to change."

When I told my longtime friend, Pete, I had no place to go for Thanksgiving, he invited me to his mother's in New Rochelle. Yay! I had swum in her condo pool the last few summers. I liked her and she liked me.

Pete's sister, whom I also liked, was there with her husband and two young sons. She and her mother bickered constantly. About the kids, the food, how to serve it, and when. The tension filled the air throughout the meal. When they weren't going at it, they bad-mouthed each other to Pete and me, whispering things they disliked.

I got to be the good daughter here.

After dinner, I called my parents. When my father heard my voice, he started to cry. "I'm sorry you're not here. I should have overpowered your mother."

I didn't ask if Mom wanted to speak to me. Too vulnerable, I had to protect myself from her "What about?"

At home the following Monday during dinner, I said to my daughter, then eleven, "No matter where you are living and what's going on in your life, you can always come home for Thanksgiving, for anything."

"What if I'm in a cult?" she asked.

"Bring your robe. I'll wash it."

I started to see Pete without his mother. Years ago, he and I had been in the same circle of friends when we had spouses and a circle. After our divorces, we became each other's sounding boards.

Pete had a pattern of falling for married women. They went back to their husbands after two to six months with Pete. Then he'd call me. When neither of us was otherwise engaged, he showed up for holidays or part of a weekend, or for functions where having an escort beat going alone.

He never called us a "we." Neither did I. Pete became a sometimes, sort-of, on again, off again beau.

That worked.

Sometimes.

When an essay I wrote about being a divorced mother was accepted at *Parents Magazine*, I got a contract saying I would be paid $1500. I thought they put in an extra zero by mistake.

"Better cash it fast," said my father when I told him.

A few days after I received the contract, the editor-in-chief, Margo, called. When she told me her name, my heart beat faster. Was she apologizing for the money mistake? Had the acceptance been a mistake?

"Nancy Kelton, Nancy Kelton," she said. "I know your name. How?"

I'd recently had a piece on being a mother published on the op-ed page of *The New York Times*. I asked if she read it.

"No, but you sent me something when I was at *New*

York, didn't you?"

Not just something. Margo had been the articles editor of *New York* for many years. I submitted many article proposals to her. "I did," I told her.

"Remind me what you sent."

I took a deep breath. "Ten article proposals."

"Right. I rejected them all, didn't I?"

Oy! "Yes."

"This is just great, Nancy."

"Great?" I said.

"You keep going. You're a pro."

A short time after that, Margo published two more of my essays. One, on my relationship with Robert, generated many letters, not all favorable, some from the Bible Belt. She called and read me a few, saying that they would appear in an upcoming issue.

"Does that kind of mail upset you?" I asked.

Margo laughed. "Are you kidding? I'm thrilled. I'm actually calling to see if you'd have lunch with me on Friday."

I had met Margo a few years earlier at the Marymount Writers Conference where we were both panelists. Our lunch at Hatsuhana was not like a blind date.

Au contraire. My lunch with Margo was Heaven.

"I'd like you to write more essays for *Parents.* How's four a year?" she said.

It only takes one, Dad loved to say. "Wonderful!"

Margo told me to propose each in a letter with a two-paragraph lead followed by several paragraphs explaining where I'd go. "They can be about your experiences as a single mother, on dates, with your family, anything you want. I'm not assigning an articles editor to you. I'll work with you directly."

All that. And sushi, too.

We talked and ate, not noticing that a nearby table collapsed. Dishes and glasses fell and broke. Broken pieces scattered onto the floor. Our waiter and the hostess moved our food and us to an empty table in the next room.

I marveled at how Margo picked herself up, continuing our conversation unfazed by the move and the mess. No wonder she steered the ship. She had the stuff to be at the helm.

After lunch, at her request, I walked her to her office for back issues. Pictures of her husband and three children lined her windowsills. Her corner office faced the East River and Roosevelt Island.

"I should write a profile of you and how well you juggle everything," I said.

Margo, glancing at the photos, chuckled. "It looks that way, doesn't it?"

Her husband called. She told him she'd get back to him as soon as she checked the train schedule. When she hung up, she said, "We have to decide who's driving the kids up to our house in Rhinebeck later. Our middle one's bringing a friend. We can't fit six people in our car. One of us has to take the train. It's a problem."

I considered myself a lucky lady with my great new gig

and editor. Still, I wished my biggest problem heading into a weekend was: We have no room in the car for our family and a guest, so who's taking the train to the country house?

A few years later, Margo became the president of the company and a new editor-in-chief took over. Margo missed editing and quit to become the editor-in-chief of another magazine which didn't use essays and had nothing to do with mothering or women. I continued to write for *Parents*.

Though I didn't work with her again, we remained friendly. The first time we met for dinner, she said, "Put it this way, I'm not a Rockefeller, but between my severance package and my current salary, I could send my three children to college and keep the country house and the co-op on my own." The next time I saw her, she told me she was getting divorced.

"I'm shocked," I said. "I envied you and your life."

"It worked on some cylinders for a while." One of her children was on probation from school for cheating. Another turned to drugs. "I can't think about men or dating yet, but the next time we get together, you can tell me how to go about it."

"Sure," I said. "First I have to figure it out."

We didn't have a next time. Margo got cancer. I heard from friends that after her divorce, she became very ill.

When I got home from Margo's funeral, I called Wendy.

"You used to envy Margo. You said she had it all," Wendy reminded me.

"It looked that way."

"You say that about your friend, Irene, too."

"She does."

"Nobody has it all," Wendy said.

I decided to call Ben, the good kisser with the camel coat. I figured that he'd be happy to hear from me and had probably not moved on.

I was right. We met for dinner at Charlie Mom's at 11th Street and Sixth Avenue and got right into discussing movies, books, and plays. Ben and I had the kind of conversation that came easily to New Yorkers even if they hadn't read the book or seen the show. I once attended a dinner party at which six people discussed a new Philip Roth book. None had read it. All read the reviews.

Ben and I split pan-fried noodles with shrimp, mooshu vegetables, and the check.

Heading up Sixth Avenue, he put his arm around me. It didn't repulse me, but it didn't make me want to get close. But loneliness was loneliness. And the voices of my mother and all the others who loved telling me "You've got to give people a chance. You're too picky" loomed large.

Too picky or not picky enough?

Ben asked if he could come up to my apartment. I didn't say no. On my sofa, he kissed me. Good, good. I did not want to go further, though. I still liked his kisses. I still didn't like Ben.

One Friday Wendy called to say she did not feel like

walking the following morning. Her husband had moved out. Being Wendy, she didn't feel like discussing it. She asked me for the names of divorce lawyers, began interviewing them, and found one she liked.

I had a share in a single-parent beach house in Fair Harbor again and invited her out for a weekend in August. I didn't know beforehand that she and I had the same royal blue Anne Cole bathing suit. I knew we didn't have the same thighs.

As we changed into our swimsuits, a scene from the summer I was thirteen flashed through my mind. At my urging, my pretty friend, Sally, came to Camp Tamakwa where I had spent three summers. Following dinner on the first night, the Spartans, a group of cool boys who didn't know I existed the previous summers, now surrounded me. How was I, they wanted to know. How was my year? And by the way, who was my cute friend?

Sally spent the summer in the boathouse with the boyfriend she picked out. I spent mine saving drowning victims in Junior Life Saving.

And wondering why I wanted Sally at my camp.

Why, I now wondered, staring at Wendy's perfect thighs, had I invited her to the beach?

Wendy also stared at her thighs. And at everything else below eye level. For the rest of the weekend, she barely looked up or spoke. On the dock at sunset, I mingled. Wendy stayed back at the house. After dinner, a neighbor had a party. I went and danced. Wendy stayed at the house. Afterwards, my housemates and I played Charades. Wendy played for a short while. Then she petered out.

"I can't put myself out there the way you do," she said on the ferry Sunday night. "I don't have that muscle. I can't do it."

Can't or won't? I still did not get that about people. Was it can't or won't?

Wendy had a lunch date with a cute, very young buyer who came to her showroom. On their second date, they played tennis. She liked him.

But at the beginning of September, her husband moved home. "Marriage is easier," she said on our next Saturday walk. "No man will love me or my kids the way he does. Besides, I'm better off with the devil I know than a new one."

My mother once said that people stayed married to have someone there for the holidays. Of course. The holidays sucked.

According to Chris Rock, married people want to kill each other and single people want to kill themselves. I understood that too.

I no longer wished I had Wendy's thighs. I wished I knew what I wanted. I wished I didn't feel so rotten on holidays. I wished my husband or Robert had been My Guy.

Ben continued to call. I didn't see him, but I liked having someone to talk to right before going to sleep.

I liked Ben on the phone.

I told him I would be taking Emily to my parents' condo in Pembroke Pines, Florida, during her school break. Ben's aunt lived in Pembroke Pines. He decided to visit her while we'd be there.

It seemed like an okay idea. In New York. On the phone.

It meant that I would not have to get out of the pool at three o'clock every day to rush for the early bird special. And I could talk about something other than the next meal.

More important, my parents might stop worrying about me, about my lack of companionship and my being a loser, about my going through life alone. In Florida, so would I.

My mother fell all over Ben when he picked me up for dinner. My mother fell over every Jewish lawyer who ever appeared at our house to take my sister or me out.

Before getting into his car, Ben wanted to see the grounds. I showed him the pool and tennis courts. He had on a short-sleeved aqua and yellow flowered shirt, which on a sexy, virile guy would have been cool. On Ben's oddly shaped body, it hung loose and looked awful. I wasn't sure if any article of clothing suited Ben other than his camel cashmere coat.

We walked beyond the pool area to the little beach at the artificial lake. Ben put his arm around me, turned me towards him, and kissed me.

I tried pulling away, but he did not let me. He wanted another kiss.

"How about we go for dinner now?" I said.

"How about we get married?"

Huh?

Still gazing into my eyes, he said, "Marry me. You could do worse."

I smiled. "I don't think so."

Fortunately, he laughed. We went to a deli in Fort Lauderdale. Neither of us mentioned his proposal. Or the kiss. Or whether we should go Dutch treat. In the spirit of friendship and as an apology for my glib response to his proposal, I picked up the check.

We said goodnight at the door of my parents' apartment. They were asleep with their bedroom door closed. No lights were on in the living room and sleeping alcove, but Emily, on one of the two couches, which we made up as beds at night, was awake.

"We saw you walk to the lake, Mom. What did you do there?"

"Not much."

Her half-opened eyes kept closing. "How was your date?"

"Not great." For a few seconds, I felt like I was in my college dorm, giving my half-sleeping roommate a late-night date report. Those conversations, like this, were more connected and more fun than the dates.

I sat down on the bed beside my daughter. The pale green lightweight blanket was down around her feet. "Want me to turn on the air conditioner, sweetie?" I felt her forehead to see if she was hot.

"No. I was hot before. I'm not now."

I pulled the blanket up to her waist. She put her hands over it. That was where she liked her blanket on warm nights. At her waist. A few strands of her long blonde hair were on her cheek. I pushed them back. "Ben asked me to marry him."

She opened her eyes. Wide. "And?"

"I said 'no'."

"Good." She turned over and fell asleep.

I thought so, too. Admittedly, I was lonely. But desperate? Nuh uh.

And no way would I settle. I realized that in Florida when Ben, who looked like he was on a coat hanger, proposed by the artificial lake.

Part Five

After the Early Bird Dinners

For twenty minutes before my father's funeral, as people I'd never met and relatives I didn't like congregated in the lobby and family room of the funeral home, I stayed in the chapel, staring at him in his size 39-Short navy blazer with a light blue dress shirt and paisley tie underneath. Along with gray slacks or khakis, this was his special occasion outfit.

Two months ago, on his eighty-eighth birthday, he bounced out of his Florida bedroom all spiffed up in these clothes to go out for dinner. "Won't I make a fine-looking corpse?" he asked.

He had asked that question before in these clothes. Each time, I got the willies, terrified of life on this planet without him, but I laughed because he laughed, because he so wanted adoration, because, as always, the spark in his eyes was dancing, and because he encouraged laughter in the face of everything.

Victor, the funeral director, appeared with the two ratty decks of cards I'd brought: one said United Airlines, the other First Bank of Buffalo. I placed them in the coffin. No more gin rummy or casino with me. No more twinkle in Dad's eyes now shut for eternity. Just darkness. Blackness. A void.

I sat down in the front row. How surreal! My mother had been the sick one. No question, she'd die first. Then Dad got pneumonia. And was now "a fine-looking corpse."

Did he die to get away from her? Had he had enough?

Not really. Not exactly. Not consciously, anyhow. On his birthday, I sat with him at the condo pool. He waved to his cronies, all younger and less robust than he. A few used walkers. One had cancer, another, a bad heart.

"What's your secret, Dad?"

"No secret. I don't want to be sick. I've got more Social Security to collect. It comes with." He smiled. "I want to outlive your mother so I'll know what real peace is."

Ten years earlier, Mom's doctor found an aortic aneurysm during her routine physical and scheduled surgery the following week at the Miami Heart Institute. I flew down. When the anesthesiologist examined her, he heard wheezing. The surgery was postponed.

That evening as my father and I walked out of the hospital, he looked as frightened and as sad as I'd ever seen him. He handed me the car keys. He rarely let me drive. For the first five minutes in the car, he was silent. Then he said, "I should have known in 1935 when I was courting her and we were necking on her parents' living room sofa what I was getting into. She'd breathe real heavy. I thought it was passion. It wasn't passion. It was her asthma."

Somewhere he knew. Somewhere we know the person we marry, or have a glimpse; but for more than one reason, some not in our awareness, we see what we want, look the other way, pretend it doesn't matter, and live with the person's difficult parts, because they work for us, because we don't know better, because water finds its level or the other person's difficult parts fit with ours, and because they 'come with.'

On the Miami Heart Institute forms we were required to fill out before Mom's surgery, pages of ailments were listed alphabetically. We had to check off those she had.

"Acid reflux, allergies, aneurysm, angina, arteriosclerosis, asthma," Dad said, checking them all. "We haven't even gotten to the Bs."

We had. Decades before with her breakdown.

Mom's surgery, a success, was followed by dementia and several falls. Her most recent, a month ago, resulted in a broken pelvis. Recovering in a Florida nursing home rehab unit, she had no clue Daddy died.

Two weeks ago he got pneumonia. His internist and the covering doctor were both vacationing. The coverer twice-removed admitted him to a rinky-dink, local hospital. He told Mom he had a cold.

I flew down.

On the third day, his pneumonia got worse. The pulmonary specialist who examined him seemed more inept than the coverer twice-removed. Dad's regular doctor returned from vacation. Very tan. He got updated. Without consulting me and my sister, who had arrived, he told my father he might not make it. A rabbi appeared.

A relative whom Dad disliked – Fred, I'll call him – visited. Dad chatted with him, even asked for his help with the *Times* puzzle. When Fred headed to the hospital cafeteria, my father turned to me, smiling the sweetest smile. "Nice guy," he said.

Huh! Then I got it! My father was forgiving himself for years of slinging arrows at Fred. And forgiving Fred for being human.

He burst into "One Man and His Dog Went to Mow a Meadow," a song he'd taught me forty-five years before. It started with one man and went up to any number we wanted. We used to stop at three or four. I never knew if Dad made up the song or not, but with an oxygen tube in his nose and a twinkle in his eyes, after being told by his tan doctor he might not make it, he said, "Let's do it now." Together we sang:

One man and his dog went to mow a meadow.
One man and his dog went to mow a meadow.
Two men and their dogs went to mow a meadow.
Two men, one man, and their dogs went to mow a meadow.

Dad, putting up his hand, stopped. "I want to call Mom." He hadn't spoken to her in a week. He got through this time.

"I'm still sniffling, honey," he said. There was timber in his voice, but his eyes filled up with tears. "I'll come see you when my cold's better." He held the phone tightly. "I miss you."

He did it! Loving, singing, and forgiving. That was how he wished to leave this world. Intentional or not, I'll never know, but my father showed me how to die. And taught me how to live.

My parents, married for sixty-one years and together for sixty-five, necked on the sofa with asthma, passion and, from what I could gather as their child, ever so much more. Lucky them.

Sitting at my father's bedside while he said good-bye to his sweetheart, I felt like a third wheel.

My sister and her husband, Carl, walked into the chapel. With Susan beside me, peering inside the coffin, I ran my hand along the wooden rim.

The night before, out of respect for our beloved and frugal father, we chose the second cheapest, overpriced coffin. The least expensive pine box in the coffin room, unfinished and un-put-together, seemed too splintery and too cheap even for a Davidoff.

"It's crowded out there," Susan said. "The snow didn't keep anyone away."

Even if it hadn't snowed, we expected just a few relatives. My parents had been living in Florida for years. But *The Buffalo News* had an enormous obituary and Aunt Dora, Dad's only remaining sibling, had an enormous mouth.

When a well-liked, hometown lawyer meets his maker, death pre-empts *Meet the Press.*

I reached for Susan's hand. "Let's tell Daddy he got a good turnout."

Carl piped in, "That's not your father in there."

Geez! If he meant the body was only a body and man's essence was his soul, didn't he know I knew? Was *now* the best time to get anal? All I wanted was a moment with my size 39-Short dad.

I squeezed Susan's hand. Could she shrug off that remark? She put two books in the coffin: Alfred Sheinwald's *Five Weeks to Winning Bridge* and Mark Twain's *Letters from the Earth.*

"He's always behind something," Mom used to say when he sat on the sofa with a book, a crossword puzzle, or his cards.

Yes! But at least we could find him. At least he came out.

Carl left the chapel. My sister turned to me. "Weird,

huh?"

"That Daddy's dead or that Mom doesn't know?" I turned to her, smiling. "Or that that's not our father in there?" *Or that despite a lifetime of my longing to breathe in her air and her wanting me to get lost, we stood shoulder to shoulder now?*

I had been trying extra hard with Susan since being told that Daddy might not make it. The day before, Emily needed clothes for the funeral. I had not rented a car and Aunt Dora was out using hers. When Susan's friend drove up to take her shopping, I asked if Emily could go with them. Susan said no. I counted to ten and said nothing, picturing Dad's show of forgiveness at the end.

Susan left the chapel and an elegant woman in a stylish black wool cape came toward me, running up the aisle like a short Loretta Young on speed. Evelyn Wald. As newlyweds, she and her husband, Herb, lived upstairs from my parents on Jewett Parkway. My mother played their piano and the four of them sang. The couples became great friends. The last time chic little Evelyn rushed towards me was at my wedding in '69.

Noticing the cards in the coffin, she picked up the United Airlines deck. "Your father was a riot." A pause, then, "Herb died, you know."

I didn't. "I'm so sorry."

"Five months ago." Evelyn burst into tears. "In a hospice. It was his liver."

I didn't know about the hospice or Herb's liver. I shook my head some more.

"Your aunt said your mother's in a Florida nursing home. Does she know what's going on?"

"She broke her pelvis. We haven't told her yet."

The day before, while making funeral arrangements, I phoned my mother from Victor's office. "Put Daddy on," she said.

"He can't talk now, Ma."

"What's he doing?"

"Resting."

"How's his cold?"

"About the same," I said.

"Don't rush." Evelyn sobbed. "Losing a wonderful partner is hell. You can't imagine."

A pit formed in my stomach. I definitely couldn't.

Victor appeared with Mark, my rabbi cousin who'd be officiating. As I looked inside the coffin, I pictured my father forty-three years earlier, a little younger than I was now, running up Covington Avenue, holding the back of my bike and, little by little, letting go. "Keep pedaling, *tsatskeleh*. You can do it. You can do it without me."

How? I eventually learned to ride my bike, but how would I make it without Dad now? As Victor closed the coffin, I felt my father's soul rising. I put my hands across my chest to try to grab and hold it. Very, very close.

We take ourselves with us wherever we go. Wherever I go, please let me take my father.

I sat down in the front row between my sister and daughter, taking a breath in and letting a breath out, alternating between being too here and not here at all.

That Cousin Mark began with *Ecclesiastes* did not help. *To everything there is a season, and a time to every purpose under the heaven: A time to be born, and a time to die.* Mark had begun Aunt Yetta's funeral service and probably the funerals of his congregants for decades in the same way. I needed something less Pete Seeger-y, something personal and unique for my one and only treasure of a dad.

I turned to Eddie, Daddy's shady old buddy, directly behind me in the second row. Eddie had a history of arriving late, if he showed up at all. He used to fool around with women and with the law. My father got him reinstated when he was disbarred, and covered for him when his wife called. The two men spoke Yiddish to each other and laughed about everything and everyone. Eddie had slipped in here an hour before, his topcoat on and his hat in his hand, his head bowed. He hugged me and told me he wanted to be a pallbearer. Daddy would be thrilled his bad-boy pal was central to his send off.

He was as close as I could get to Dad.

But Mom. Absent Mom. My missing mom. I couldn't get close to her.

Or to my sister and her words now as she eulogized Dad. I felt removed from the chapel. Far away. My mother's not showing up and participating, an ache this past week and for the past forty-nine years, came over me like a tsunami. Years of therapy and work on myself all got erased. It pissed me off that she wasn't here. I longed for a mommy now.

I longed, too, to connect to Susan's words about the father I deeply loved, but like my rabbi cousin's *Ecclesiastes,* they did not engage me. Did she engage in what she said?

I got up and read my eulogy: an open letter to my father I had written eleven years before for *Parents.* My voice did not crack. I knew not to write something new.

Emily nodded as I sat down and whispered that I did well. I reached for her hand. She patted mine. Then Mark called her up. She hadn't told me she'd be speaking, but before breakfast she disappeared to a back room at Aunt Dora's house with a legal pad.

How beautiful and poised she looked as she stood before two hundred strangers. She began with the Rosalind Russell line from *Auntie Mame* she had used in her college essays: "*Life is a banquet and most poor suckers are starving to death.*" Then she said, "My Papa Max was my Auntie Mame. He wasn't a poor sucker. He didn't starve."

The rest of her eulogy was as heartfelt and sweet. In the chapel listening to her, I wasn't starving either.

My father was buried at The Holy Order of the Living. The cemetery namer should have called it The Jewish Order of the Dead. My mother's family and other families including Eddie's, from the Ukraine town of Sokolivka, bought plots together there.

My cousin handed Susan the shovel. Susan then gave it to me. I looked down as I shoveled dirt onto the coffin. The end. That unbearable sound. So final. "Good bye, Daddy." I looked down. Oh God! No!

Eddie stopped at his parents' headstones in the next row. The proximity of his dead parents comforted me. So did Eddie and his wife, Miriam, the only nonrelatives in our group. They had been at my grandmothers' funerals, my wedding, and sent flowers to Mt. Sinai after I gave birth. When my mother was in the nervous hospital, Susan, Daddy, and I ate dinner at their house. I invited them for lunch at Aunt Dora's.

When we arrived, her Mah-jongg friends were carrying platters of lox, bagels, herring, and whitefish salad to the dining room. I put more than a few slices of lox on half of a sesame bagel. Eddie, standing with me, watching, said, "*Kenahora*. Maxie would be proud of you."

Noticing my cousin Rosalie, a big plus size, beside me piling mounds of food on her plate, Eddie winked.

"You girls will have lots of work with your mother," Rosalie said to me glancing at Susan in the kitchen. "You should be able to get along." Years ago, I told Rosalie, a high school guidance counselor, how sad I was that my sister and I were not closer.

"We should?"

Rosalie nodded. "You're a writer. You're teachers. Communicators."

Yes! But work was work. And life was life. We *all* could give advice. Cousin Rosalie counseled troubled teens all day. After hours, she chowed down.

I walked over to the stove and put my arm around my sister. "When you get back from Florida, maybe you'll come to New York or I'll visit you and we can discuss where Mom will live." *Yes, maybe* going forward we'd be together constantly eating, giggling, looking at old photos, and having late-night talks.

She moved away from me. "Nancy, please. I'm not going to be available after Florida."

Would she ever be available? Would anyone?

Maybe not.

We sat *shiva* at Aunt Dora's. On Monday night, a woman named Sylvia, Dad's one-time secretary, came over with a homemade apple pie. After she stopped working fulltime, she typed for my father on Saturdays. Those mornings, Dad took extra pains getting dressed. I thought he was having an affair with Sylvia and didn't blame him. He deserved something on the side.

Anything.

But this pie-bringing Sylvia was a frumpy seventy-something-year-old woman with a fifties perm, support hose, clunky shoes, and teeth that pointed in various directions. In between telling us how Mr. D used to crack up the office staff, she spoke about her devoted "hubby" who dropped her off, would pick her up, and didn't let her drive at night.

This Sylvia did not strike me as "the other woman." For Dad. For anyone.

When she left, I called Eddie's wife. "Do you think my father played around?"

Miriam laughed. "Maxie didn't need other women. He got his kicks from Eddie. And he was too scared of your mother. Besides, when a married guy cheats, he's got to shell out money for fancy dinners and jewelry. Your father was too cheap."

On Tuesday morning, I drove Emily to the airport to go back to Haverford. "You were Papa's favorite grandchild."

"I know," she said.

She was the only one. Before heading inside the terminal, she turned and waved. That familiar lump formed in my throat. The lump I got with every goodbye since she walked through the nursery school door.

I stopped at Wegmans for a medium coffee at the café and headed up and down the aisles. One thing I missed about Buffalo besides Ted's foot long, charcoal-broiled hot dogs was this gargantuan Wegmans with its very wide aisles, and coming here with Dad.

Seeing a shopper reach for a brand-name toilet paper, he'd pull out the generic brand. "With this, you can go three more times a week," he'd say. And, as he had done at supermarkets since Mom's hospital stays forty years earlier, he'd approach strangers with, "Excuse me. I forgot my grocery list. May I borrow yours?"

At the bakery counter was a sign next to a platter of cut-up cheese Danish pastries and corn muffins: *Samples: one per customer.*

I sampled the Danish, then the muffin, then the Danish again. The man beside me gave a muffin sample to the little boy with him. The boy wanted a second piece, but the man pointed to the sign. "It says *Samples: one per customer*, Tommy. I'll buy you a muffin."

Buy?

The paying father asked the bakery counter woman to put one corn muffin in a brown bag. A different father smiled down from heaven. I resumed my breakfast samples, eating what came with.

I returned home to my neutered cat.

Chester sat by the door, purring. I picked him up and spoke to him the way people do to their pets, asking if he had been a good boy, if he missed me, and if Wendy talked to him when she gave him his nourishment each day. I opened a can of Fancy Feast tuna, his favorite, and watched my little black and white purring machine dive in.

I started to call my father to say I arrived home safely, but he no longer cared. Emily had class now. Then dinner. Then studying with her boyfriend or with her friends. A life.

The junk mail, bills, and what looked like three condolence cards were in two neat piles on my butcher-block table in the kitchen. I opened an envelope from the funeral home and pulled out a bill. From Thursday to Sunday, the undertaker walked us through the steps, showering us with kindness. Once the coffin was lowered, he stopped walking and showering and mailed this exorbitant, itemized bill.

Everything, but EVERYTHING, was a business. Hospitals. Illness. Dying. Death. Everything came with a price.

Two hours later I stood in front of my New School classroom, grateful to focus on my students. They ranged from twenty to mid-seventies and included undergraduates, professionals, waiters, artists, mothers, fathers, and retirees. Seven were repeaters, and not because they flunked. They liked to write. I liked them. It worked.

"Sorry I cancelled last week." I breathed in slowly and let it out. "My father got pneumonia. I went to Florida. He died Thursday. The funeral was Sunday in Buffalo."

A silence punctuated by a few "I'm sorrys" followed. My students' faces consoled me.

I opened my manila folder and took out their last assignment: a two-page open letter to someone, getting something off their chest. The three I read aloud were to a tyrannical boss, a longtime friend, and a wife who walked out. All were revealing and well-written. I didn't want to read any requiring lengthy criticism. Or written to moms and dads.

I moved into the evening's topic: creating a scene. "You know the deal. Show, don't tell." I talked about dialogue and telling details, reading from the works of Mary Karr and E.B. White.

My classes went well. This one, *Writing From Personal Experience,* also the title of my about-to-be-published book, was my favorite.

In college, when I decided that teaching would suit me better than sitting in an office typing forms in triplicate, I endured the necessary education classes, took the test for New York City public school certification, and taught first and second grades.

My little students were adorable. Honest. Real. But the older teachers who counted the days until retirement and spoke with disdain about the minority children, turned me off. "We're all created equal, but some of us are a little more equal, if you get my drift," my teacher-trainer whispered to me. That coupled with the outmoded curriculum and custodial chores – collecting milk money, cleaning up spilled paint, cleaning up the spilled candy and soda they weren't supposed to have in class, getting knots out of shoelaces and fingers out of noses – took the zing out of me.

Teaching writing put the zing back. My classes were not compulsory. My students chose to be here. My first New School class began the night after my marriage ended. Then, now, and in between, I felt grateful for this work.

"For next week, write two pages on a place where you feel comfortable," I said. "It can be a room, a house, a vacation spot, anywhere."

A place where I feel comfortable: in front of a classroom. Here.

After class, a longtime student, Sara, who at forty just got married, came up to my desk. "I'm so sorry about your father. I know from your writing how special he was."

My students and I knew each other through our writing. I knew Sara adored her older brother and had a string of bad relationships until she turned thirty-nine.

We rode down in the elevator together. "If you'd like a drink or coffee, I'll take you," she said at the 12th Street entrance.

"Thanks, Sara." I looked at her dark bob, not a hair out of place, and her bright red nails that matched her bright red lipstick. She did public relations for a music company, enjoyed her work, and had no agenda here. She just liked to write. "I have to get home," I said. *Why?*

She smiled. "Let me know if I can do anything."

Do? If Sara weren't paying for *my* guidance, she could teach *me* how to get close to my older sibling and how to find a great man.

"Thank you. I'm fine." *Lie. Lie. Lie. Lie. Lie.*

Before going to sleep, I prayed that tomorrow my father would call to say his death had been a bad dream. The first night alone after my husband left, I'd prayed he would call the next day and we would kiss and make up.

Life did not return to how it used to be. Then or now.

The next night Pete, my sometimes sort-of beau, took me to Steak Frites down the block from my building. When his last fling with a married woman ended a few months earlier, we decided this time to remain just friends.

"How would you like your filet mignon?" our waiter asked me.

"Medium." I rarely ate meat, but steak had been my father's favorite. I wanted steak tonight.

Another waiter served two rib eyes to the two men at the next table. I burst into tears. "It's the first time I've cried since we passed the shovel at the grave."

"I didn't shed one tear at my father's funeral or after," Pete said. "Not a single tear."

He droned on about his father. *His* dead father. I attended the funeral a decade ago, and heard before and after what a prick he had been. Tonight Pete made me think of the mothers who visited after I gave birth. They brought adorable outfits and stuffed animals for Emily. They replayed every boring detail of their labors from the first contraction through delivery for me.

"My book will be out next week." I cut into my steak and cut Pete off. "Will you come to a reading?"

"If I can." Pete rarely said yes right away.

"I'm doing one at the Chelsea Barnes & Noble and another at the Jefferson Market Library. Feel free to bring people."

"Your last one at the library attracted a bunch of weirdos."

"So you and your people will fit in again."

Pete studied each piece of rib eye he put in his mouth, savoring the taste as he chewed. His focus on his food and himself did not surprise or bother me. I wanted nothing from Pete other than an occasional meal. Clarity helped. About the yeses and the nos.

"I'll call you for the schedule and come to one," he said.

Walking to my building, I put my arm through his. Pete was a decent-enough man. Decent-enough did not cut it if I wanted a forever guy. Hadn't my mother – my mother of all people – stressed the importance of that 'glue?' At the door, I hugged Pete. Even in heavy overcoats, I felt his stomach protrude.

"Better I don't come up tonight, right?" he said.

I nodded. Better he didn't come up any night, anymore.

My sister went to Florida to tell Mom that Dad died. She called me from the nursing home. "I held her hand. She just listened. Then she said, 'Too bad.'"

Too bad? "She didn't seem shocked or cry or anything?" I asked.

"No," Susan said. "I couldn't tell if it registered, though."

Right. "Does Mom want to speak to me?" I asked.

"Hang on. I'll see."

I heard my sister say, "Mom, Nancy's on the phone." She said "Nancy" twice more, then, "Mom, do you want to talk to Nancy?"

My mother said what she always said. "What about?"

This time I laughed.

My book *Writing From Personal Experience* was published. At many stores, it was in the writing department shelved alphabetically by the author's last name. After mine was Kelly's *How to Write Erotica*.

"Buy the right book," I told my classes. "We'll discuss two chapters each week."

In my NYU class, my student, John, raised his hand. "So you're saying your book is required reading?"

"No. I'm saying my book is required buying."

I heard titters. People often weren't sure if I was serious or kidding. Thank God!

I ate at Steak Frites with Wendy two nights after dinner there with Pete. My choice again.

"Your father would be thrilled I'm treating," Wendy said.

"Treating and listening." Eating with Wendy comforted me. Evenings with the girls beat evenings with the boys.

Wendy gave the waiter her credit card and put on a long gray cardigan from her latest line. At our building, the doorman told us to have a good night. Wendy and I often joked that the building staff, seeing us together all these years, probably thought we were a gay couple. At the fortieth birthday party she threw for me, a friend said our body language was more in sync than that of most couples.

Wendy got into the elevator. I lived on two. She did not.

"I finished *Vogue* and a bunch of others," she said. "You can take them."

"I'll get them Saturday after our walk."

"We're going out to our house this weekend. C'mon up now. I brought you home a sweater set."

I couldn't tell if Wendy really brought me sweaters or felt sorry for me. I didn't care. I rode up with her. Inside her apartment, she disappeared to her storage room, once her daughters' bedroom. I sat on the bench of her baby grand and played "Both Sides Now."

Something's lost and something's gained in living every day.

Joni Mitchell had that one right. Losses changed us. Sometimes for the better. Sometimes not.

Wendy's mahogany piano dominated the living room. The track lighting above, coupled with the arrangement of her furniture – a cocktail table from the fifties, her mother's dining room set, modern gray loveseats, and abstract paintings by friends leaning against walls, not hung – gave her place a cool aura. Very Wendy. Very "not me."

She emerged with a beige cardigan and matching sleeveless shell, the same set she gave me in black two months before. I wore the black set all the time. "Try these," she said.

I looked at the label. A small. "I don't need to. They'll fit. I'll wear them Monday."

Yawning, she turned off the lights in the front. "Call me after class. I want to know how you looked." She ushered me to the door.

Sometimes I wished Wendy and I were a couple. I could do worse. I have.

"Do you feel special that your father appointed you the executrix?" Mildred asked at my next session.

I shook my head. A part of me *did* feel special, but at these prices, why waste time sharing good stuff? "It's depressing and upsetting. He could have named Susan, too."

When I started therapy years ago, I discussed my mother and how I wanted to be one. I brought new issues to Mildred now: one dead parent, another not all there, and a sister who spent much of her time in the lotus position.

"He could have, but he didn't. Didn't you tell me Susan doesn't like numbers and dealing with money?"

I nodded. "She's older, though."

Mildred stared at me, taking in what I said and what I omitted, putting it together as carefully as she put together herself. I had been going round and round on my father not naming both my sister and me to be co-executrixes. Guilt! Guilt! Guilt!

"He appointed you. He trusted you," Mildred said. "She probably wouldn't have wanted the job."

"It's a lot of work for one person," I said.

"What isn't a lot of work, Nancy?" Mildred stood up and got two tissues from the tissue box on the table next to me. She took off her glasses and wiped them.

"But his appointing me makes my sister hate me more."

Had I earned Dad's trust because I got it? Or had I learned to get it because I took after him? Was it nature or nurture? The chicken or the egg?

The development of family bonds remained a mystery to me.

Mildred's piercing eyes penetrated my soul. Her steeliness did not scare me. I felt the tenderness and empathy at her core. The moment I sat down in her office twenty years ago for our first session, I began to let it out. I had planned to discuss a magazine article I could not begin because of writer's block. What poured out was, "When my mother came home from the mental institution, I was afraid to kiss her because I didn't think she'd want to kiss me back. I rushed downstairs anyway, thinking that was silly, of course she would. My instincts had been right: she wasn't happy to see me. She didn't kiss me back. 'I'm tired,' she said. 'It's been a long ride.' Then she moved past me."

With Mildred, I let it hang out. Finally, I was safe.

She continued now, "Your father could have considered Susan's feelings. That wasn't your father." A pause then, "Your problems with your sister didn't just start. She doesn't want to be best buddies, Nancy." Mildred spoke my name when she made a strong point, when she said something I needed to hear. And change. "Be thankful you have people you're close to." Mildred's buzzer rang. "We have to stop."

Standing up, my eyes went from her freshly highlighted hair to the hump on her back. A dowager's hump. I had not seen that before. Mildred, once my height, was shorter now. My shrink was shrinking. During a session when I wondered out loud if I'd be in therapy with her forever, she said, "I promise you we're not going to grow old together, Nancy."

Apparently not. She was getting there faster.

I turned the knob and opened the door. A first. Talk about progress. Until this moment, Mildred ushered me out.

"My apartment feels so empty," I said. "It's depressing there."

"I know. This is a rough time for you. Your father occupied a lot of space in your life, Nancy." Then in a quieter voice, she said, "Too much."

The best part about being on a plane: you can't do much about your problems.

You can't always do much about them on the ground either, but in the air there's no point in trying so you might as well enjoy the ride. My seatbelt was fastened, the take-off smooth. The captain reported that it was eighty-one and sunny in Fort Lauderdale.

At least the weather would be great.

I started to unfold my *Times,* but put it in the seat pocket and closed my eyes. As a new mother, I used to fall asleep on the sofa with my clothes on after putting Emily to bed. The same thing began happening when I got home from the health club after an hour of high impact aerobics and an hour of body stretch classes. Neither exhausted me the way grieving now did.

I drifted off. In my dream, my mother sat in her wheelchair on a stage in a huge auditorium, saying whatever came to mind, cracking up the entire SRO audience. My father, sitting in the front row center, laughed harder than anyone except for the man beside him who happened to be Bob Hope. I did not understand why everyone found Mom amusing. Or why she had two funny men in the palm of her hand when I did not have one.

The plane ride became bumpy. I opened my eyes. My seatmate, a plump, strawberry blonde, late fifties judging from her lined face, pulled a red thermos from her tote bag, took a swig, and resumed reading her *Good Housekeeping.*

The captain turned on the "fasten seatbelt" sign. "Folks, it might get very rocky."

Oh Captain, my captain! It's been rocky for so long. Fifty-two years, with an occasional time out. I put my seat in an upright position. Turbulence. The turbulence between New York and Florida was in my stomach now. I clutched it, then the armrest. "It's like a bus ride in the air," I mumbled.

My seatmate chuckled. "That's cute." Opening her thermos again, she took another swig. "Bloody Marys. You want?"

I shook my head. "I have to drive." A pit formed in my stomach. My father would not be waiting at the airport in front of the others. Excited. Beaming. I would never again call him with my flight information and hear him say, "We'll be there."

My seatmate shrugged. "Driving never stops me. My husband's probably loaded, too." She finished every last drop. "At forty-two, I should do what I want."

Forty-two? Only forty-two! Does every dog have its day? As a child, I thought college was life's great equalizer. The equalizers changed. Marriage. Children. Divorce. Disappointments. Old age if we get lucky. Then a quick or drawn out end game.

Time evened everything out. Peggy Sue got married. The prom queens lost their crowns. If not during childhood, then after the prom, life messed with us all.

My mother was not in the wheelchair line-up of rehab

patients in the hallway outside their doorways. Or in her room. Her hearing aid case with both hearing aids was on her night table next to an empty half-pint container of skim milk with a bent straw in the hole. On her unmade bed was a tray of dirty plates. On the smallest plate were chocolate crumbs.

The empty bed by the window was made with freshly ironed white sheets. No clothes or dishes were on that side. My mother's roommate must have gone home, back to the hospital, or died. At the nurses' station, an aide I knew said my mother was in the lounge.

"Sorry about your father," said the security guard, leaning against the desk, pointing me in the right direction. "He liked kidding around."

The guard used to get Dad a wheelchair. The walk to my mother's room tired him out. Heading to it with him through this hallway, his bald spot coupled with the palpable silence that replaced the conversations we had had my whole life choked me up more than visiting Mom.

Now in the lounge with two other residents, a male and female both in hospital gowns, watching, or at least looking in the direction of the television mounted on the wall, she smiled when she saw me. "There you are."

"Hi, Mom." I sat down and reached over to kiss her.

She wiped it off. "It's about time. Do you know how long I've been waiting for you?"

I didn't. Neither did she, but I've learned not to respond. "You look good." She did.

"Real good," she said.

She seemed more relaxed than she had been as a condo shut-in. Her short white hair smelled freshly shampooed. She wore Dad's navy cardigan over a yellow jersey and brown cotton slacks with an elastic waistband. The red flowered pocketbook that she took everywhere was on her lap with the handle on her wrist. She bought me the same pocketbook. It was on the top shelf of my hall closet still in the Burdines bag.

"You do, Mom." I stroked her hair. Her cute choppy cut framed her face better than the longer, all-one-length-dyed-red hairdo she had for a zillion years. "Your hair's more stylish than when it was teased and sprayed and colored."

She laughed. "You're the one who looks good." She gave me the once-over, her eyes resting on my orange tee shirt. "That's better than the dreary clothes you usually wear."

"I try." At the condo, I changed out of my brown v-neck to avoid remarks about my dreary clothes that turned me into an eleven-year-old.

Two waitresses emerged from the dining room laughing. My mother scrunched up her face.

"Should we go to your room, Mom?"

"I don't have a room," she shot back. "I've been waiting for you. If you're not taking me to your house, I'll go to Jewett Parkway with Ma."

Jewett Parkway. The street on which my mother grew up. Grandma Cohen stayed in the Jewett house until she died. Was that where Mom wanted to live? In the past?

With Grandma? Was reuniting with Mother a universal longing at the end?

Her eyes stayed on me. Should I mention Dad?

I moved closer. Her teeth were yellowing. She had spaces on the top. I put my hand on her knee. "Mom, I know Susan told you about Daddy."

She did not move my hand. "What a shame!" Her voice and face showed no affect. She opened her pocketbook, feeling her compact and lipstick, making sure they were there. She peered at me again. In a distant formal tone she said, "My condolences to you."

To me? Was that her dementia talking? Or was it what she thought a well-mannered lady should say? Didn't she feel an attachment to Dad? In her eyes, was I his mate?

I took a deep breath. "Condolences to you, Mom. Daddy adored you."

Her eyes lit up. "You think so?" She looked at me as if I were the grownup and she the child begging for The Truth.

"I know so. You two were lucky."

She nodded. "He was a natural, your dad. You take after him." She turned to the television, then to me. "He wasn't happy. Not with me here. If I'd been home, he wouldn't have caught a cold." A pause. "I thought the poor guy ran off to the woods with a young girl."

I burst out laughing. "He didn't, Mom. We had a funeral."

"Oh!" She seemed surprised. "Sadie and Jack didn't come, did they?"

"No." My great Aunt Sadie and Uncle Jack died decades

ago. "Other relatives showed up."

She went on. "Sadie and Jack don't visit me here. They're on a cruise. Not to the Caribbean this time." She stopped, as if something dawned on her. "They went to the other place. You know where?"

"I think so."

Her favorite aide Dolores appeared, spoke to the other patients, and changed the television channel to *Oprah*, then waved to us as she wheeled the man to the restroom.

"She's done well for a colored girl," Mom said.

I think she meant Oprah, not Dolores. "Do you like her show?"

"No. The guy before her was better." She rolled her hand. "What's his name?"

"Daddy?"

She laughed again. "Not Daddy." She rolled her hand some more. "Merv. No. Not Merv. Phil. Phil Donahue. I liked him. Didn't you?"

"You bet!" Through my thirties I'd let her know my taste was different and hipper than hers. No need anymore.

Dolores wheeled the man back to his spot and headed over with outstretched arms. "Nice you girls are catchin' up." She hugged Mom, then me.

"It sure is," I said. "And nice to see my mother looking healthy."

Mom patted Dolores' arm. "Marge here takes good care of me."

"It's easy. You're fun," Dolores sat beside her. "Esther, tell Nancy what you told me before." She giggled.

"You tell her, Marge." My mother has been calling her favorite aides, at home and now here, "Marge." The original Marge, a caring neighbor, used to visit daily with baked goods.

Dolores looked from Mom to me. "She says she wants a man to neck around with."

Didn't we all! "Cool, Ma! Any prospects here?"

She flicked her wrist. "They're too old. And that guy in my room wasn't my type."

Maybe because her roommate was a woman. An honest mistake. The curtain between their beds was rarely open. They never conversed. An occasional glimpse of the woman's slicked-back ducktail hair style – what we called a D.A. or Duck's Ass in the 1950s – and facial hair might have made even someone without dementia think the room had gone co-ed.

"I know." I rubbed my hand along her arm. "If you find someone, see if he has a brother."

"Don't you have boyfriends?" she asked.

"Not exactly." Not wanting pity, I added, "I've had a few."

"Daddy," she said.

Daddy again. Ouch! Hadn't her indifference and illness driven me to him?

Dolores glanced at the clock. "Naptime, Esther. How 'bout we go to your room?"

My mother shook her head. "I'm leaving." Then to me, "Aren't you taking me with you?"

"We'll talk about it," I said.

She shook her head again. "No talk. Please. No talk. That guy in my room left here without any talk. His son came, packed him up, and off they went."

I turned to Dolores. "Where to?"

"Her son's house. He and his family live in Lauderdale."

"Isn't that a good son?" Mom said.

Is there room for my mother at the good son's?

"I'll see you girls later," Dolores said. She pointed to the woman watching *Oprah*. "I have to take her to the nurse now. I'm off tomorrow, but we'll discuss everything the day after."

"Only you won't, Marge," Mom said. "Call me at Nancy's. That's where I'm going and that's where I'll live."

Is there room at the good son's for me?

At five o'clock, I had the condo pool to myself except for two gray-haired women in dark bathing suits with skirts who waded in the shallow end. One held a flutter board and kicked. The other, standing next to her, moved her hands and mouth. She talked about the broiled red snapper, stuffed jumbo shrimp, and veal scaloppini she and her cronies ate for their early bird dinner the night before. And about the omelet with Swiss cheese and spinach she thought she might cook for herself this evening while heating the mushroom barley soup from Sunday night. They may have been discussing *Anna Karenina* when I was at the deep end, but each time I swam by them, the talker gave the kicker the details of her meals.

Will I be wading with the girls at their age in a skirted

bathing suit? Will I talk or kick? Will I still be swimming laps? Will I still be here?

Under the clubhouse awning, three men sitting together all got up to leave. Abe Pearlstein, my father's bridge buddy and the only one I knew, seeing me wave, walked over with his cane. We shook hands. "Sorry about your father. Fast, wasn't it?" Not waiting for my answer, Abe continued, "Was it his heart?"

"Pneumonia," I said, my throat constricting. Grief blindsided me. Who knew what did Dad in? Mis-medication? Negligence? Stupidity? Exhaustion? Didn't more than one thing get us in the end?

"I miss him," Abe Pearlstein said. "He was my favorite bridge partner."

"He said the same thing about you," I told him. Actually, my father said Abe Pearlstein was his worst part-ner in sixty-some years of playing bridge and the only one who ever trumped his ace. I pulled over a lounge chair for him. "Come. Sit down, Mr. Pearlstein."

He shook his head. "My wife's waiting. At five-thirty, dinner's on the table. My wife made meatloaf. My favorite."

"Mine, too." I liked my meatloaf, liked seasoning it and playing with the raw ground beef. I missed making meatloaf for the people I loved and eating the leftovers cold on Kaiser rolls the next day. I missed family meals.

I gave Mr. Pearlstein a peck on the cheek. "Maybe I'll see you down here tomorrow."

Opening the gate, he let in a woman with her mother, a longtime resident, in a wheelchair. Last year at the pool,

Mom pointed them out. "The old lady's in her nineties and that's her daughter, Fran, pushing her around. She gave up her life in New York to move down here."

Fran wheeled her mother to the shallow end, locked the brake, and headed down the pool steps. I sat on the edge, dangling my feet in the water.

"Isn't it peaceful here now?" I said.

The good daughter nodded. "Looks like we'll have another great sunset." A pause, then, she said, "I remember your father. Max. He'd come down here alone and read or find an audience." She turned towards the wheelchair, smiling, "That's my mother."

"I know." I told her where mine was and that I had to figure out where she would live. "Last year she pointed you out. She wants me to be you."

"I'm hardly a saint." Fran splashed water on her face and shoulders. "My mother's easy. And in good health. Her apartment's huge. I worked for an optometrist and had a tiny apartment in Queens. I have it better here." She dunked. "I never really talked to your parents. I'm always with her." Waving to her mother who waved to her, she headed up the pool steps. "I wish I could hang out, but it's time to make dinner."

"You cook every night?"

"Every meal." She dried off with a large orange and yellow towel. "You'll figure it out."

Having my mother live with me would be a stretch. No. Having my mother live with me would drive me insane. Still, overhearing Fran describe how she'd bake the flounder they bought that morning and maybe make a green salad, I envied her contentment.

Did Fran get what life was *really* about?

How could I take care of my mother? I had a daughter, work, and friends up north. Did that or didn't *that* count? The truth: I was not a Fran.

She was one of the lucky ones, though. Her purpose seemed so clear.

I watched her push the wheelchair to the gate. Did she ever want to push it into the pool?

The pool attendant wearing a University of Miami sweatshirt walked around folding umbrellas. He waved. A college sophomore, majoring in European History, he mentioned during my last visit that he worked here to earn money for his upcoming junior year in Spain.

"Anything you need?" asked the cute attendant, standing over my lounge chair.

Everything. "No thanks," I said.

"You're shivering. There are saunas in the locker rooms and a co-ed Jacuzzi just inside."

"I know, but I'm going back to the apartment in a few minutes." *Why?* Considering I had no one to talk to and no food in the fridge, I didn't know what I would do there other than get into dry clothes, go eat at some deli, return and get the willies deciding whether I should sleep on one of the two couches in the alcove, or in my parents' bedroom in my parents' bed.

"I'm just about finished working for today," he said. "I'll probably use the Jacuzzi." He smiled.

I smiled back.

Did he smile the same way at Abe Pearlstein and the two ladies in bathing suits with skirts? Or was he flirting? Was I?

This was not the right time. The pool attendant was not the right guy, but in the future, I might wish to flirt. In the future, I'd like to do more than flirt.

"I'm going to take a hot shower and snuggle up in my robe," I told him. Robe? What robe? I didn't have a robe here. What was with me? Volunteering my plans for the evening? Using words like "snuggle up?" I sounded like a cougar. Pathetic. Ick.

The wind kicked up. I had goose bumps on my arms. I glanced around. The pool area had emptied out except for two men sitting under the clubhouse awning. They got up, too, walked together to the gate and headed in different directions. I felt like I did in seventh grade at Temple Beth Zion dance class on Saturday nights. The boys rushed across the floor to dance with the pretty girls. I stood watching, waiting to be picked.

I put on my oversized white Hanes tee shirt, wrapped my beach towel around me like a shawl, and reached into my tote bag for the condo keys.

Did everyone have someone to talk to over dinner at a restaurant or at home?

"Get warm, then," said the young pool attendant. "And have a great night."

"You too."

He moved on to fold up the rest of the umbrellas. I headed to the apartment to begin my great night.

For my fiftieth birthday, Irene treated me to five days at the Tucson Canyon Ranch. Every morning, we woke up at dawn and, in seven minutes, got washed, dressed, and over to the meeting place for the hike. At night, in our twin beds, we talked and giggled. Easy. Smooth. The surroundings, pampering, hiking, and healthy food nourished me. The best part: rooming with Irene and feeling like I did as a college junior. The bummer: our good-bye.

"We'll do this again when we turn sixty," she said at the airport as we hugged.

Whenever I talked about the future with my parents, they told me to say, "If all is well." My mother reminded me Jews didn't plan. It brought bad luck.

"If all is well," I said to Irene, clutching the sleeve of the sweater she had on her shoulders, not wanting to let go. "We'll figure out sixty when we get to sixty."

At home, Wendy took me to Japonica for my fiftieth. Louise took me to Aureole and bought me a needlepoint pillow on which it said, *Old friends are the best friends.*

She asked me to speak at the fiftieth birthday luncheon she'd be throwing for herself the following month. Oy! Speaking in front of a classroom had not made speaking elsewhere less terrifying. It touched me though, that with all Louise's friends, and she had many, she wanted me to be the entertainment.

My speech included: the nine navy, cable stitched, identical-looking sweaters knit by her mother; the seventeenth surprise birthday party she threw for me because I had not had a Sweet Sixteen; her noisy, unsafe car with the dropped muffler and bad brakes into which I'd jump when she'd call out, "Get in, get in," chugging down my street, unable to stop; her love of books she shared with my father; and her daily phone calls when my marriage ended and after my father died.

At the luncheon, my heart beat wildly as I began to speak. By my third sentence which got a laugh, my shoulders relaxed.

It helped that I had practiced for Sally, our childhood friend, who had come in from Oakland and was staying with me.

As we headed to the luncheon earlier, it started to snow.

"Let's walk backwards," Sally said.

We did. Up Park Avenue. Like we had walked along North Drive, shoveled or not, to PS #66 our first two years of elementary school: backwards in the snow.

Since my father died, she and I spoke once a week. Her voice, like Irene's, soothed me in the wee small hours. Thank goodness for my West Coast, three-hour-earlier friends.

"Your father's in a better place," Sally said on my sofa after Louise's luncheon. A Hare Krishna for fifteen years and still embracing its teachings, she believed death was not the end.

I wanted to believe that too. "Where is he?" I asked.

"I don't know, but he's watching over you, maybe hanging out with my father."

"You call hanging out with your father being in a better place?"

She laughed. After childhood, we drifted apart. Sally, the cute, blonde cheerleader/prom queen, won the hearts of boys. She and the one she married became Hare Krishnas and moved to Europe. When I visited her parents in Buffalo, it was like paying a *shiva* call. Her mother clutched her stomach. It had not gone according to her plan for Sally to marry one of her princes.

Eventually, after she got divorced and gave back the orange robe, she did.

"You know I loved my father," Sally said. "You remember how much he adored me."

Yes! And how I envied their physical connection! "Sally's father's always kissing and hugging her," I reported to Dad when I was little during a gin rummy game.

"So go kiss and hug Sally's father," he said, not looking up from his cards.

She went on now. "It's hard to explain it and too soon for you to understand, but since my dad died, I'm freer. You'll see. You'll have a new kind of freedom too."

I sort of got what Sally meant.

Clutching the pillow Louise bought me, I stared at the words: "Old friends are the best friends."

My old friends — my unofficial therapists — showed up. I loved them all.

After the fiftieth birthday celebrations, they returned to their husbands.

❖

I returned to my mother. And to deciding where she would live. Help!

Confined to a wheelchair and afraid to use a walker, she remained in the rehab unit of the Florida nursing home. My sister thought she should stay in warm, sunny Florida.

We had no family there. I thought it was a bad idea, but I visited Florida senior living facilities, anyway. Talk about depressing. Sadness on the residents' faces. I couldn't let my mother live in one of those facilities. Far away in the sunshine state.

I interviewed aides to live with her in her condo. When one did not show up and another came a half hour late, I knew I couldn't manage homecare from New York.

I checked out places in Brooklyn, Queens, Long Island, Manhattan, and Buffalo, with Susan and alone. They ranged from dreary to drearier. Some smelled. Some stank.

The Weinberg Campus, in the Buffalo suburb of Williamsville, stood out. Immaculate and bright, it was the nicest facility we saw. The staff was friendly. The food looked palatable. The residents engaged in activities and with each other. People I knew had loved ones there. Relatives lived nearby.

The waiting list was long. Getting accepted was like getting accepted to Harvard minus the SATs, but not impossible. Not like getting Mom a room at Menninger had been forty-two years before.

I called the admissions people at Weinberg once or

twice a week. A well-connected Buffalo cousin called, too.

My sister does not fly. Eventually, when a room became available, the move to Weinberg from Florida became my job. I sold my parents' Toyota to Marge, the kind neighbor. I sold my parents' Florida condo for a song. I gave away the furniture, my father's clothes, and most of my mother's.

Off to Buffalo we flew.

My Aunt Dora met us at the airport. The first words out of my mother's mouth were, "She's not that fat. You said she was fat."

"I said Cousin Rosalie was fat."

"Rosalie *is* fat. Very fat," Mom said. "A hippo. But you also said Aunt Dora was fat."

I hadn't. Thank goodness Aunt Dora laughed. I stayed at her house the next five days. And for the next three years whenever I visited my mother.

The first day at Weinberg, my mother and I spoke with the social worker. "Do you have any questions, Esther?" she asked.

"Not for you." She turned to me. "This is the old folks' home. How come you parked me in the old folks' home?"

Ouch!

For five nights, I went on and on about "parking Mom in the old folks home" with Aunt Dora at Ted's over charcoal broiled hot dogs, in her family room playing Scrabble, and in the kitchen every morning over breakfast. Back home, I discussed it with Mildred.

"What are your other choices?" Mildred asked.

On one Buffalo visit, a real estate agent showed me three houses in Williamsville. One had a pool. I could sublet or sell my New York apartment, rent or a buy a house in Buffalo, and move in with my mother and an aide.

"Is that what you want to do?" Mildred asked.

I shook my head.

Four months after my mother moved to Weinberg, she fell. They could not keep her in the assisted living facility. They moved her to the nursing care part.

I continued to visit once a month for a long weekend. My aunt and cousins visited in between. So did a onetime neighbor, Mrs. Kaplowitz. "I better not be in this place when my time comes," she told me on the phone. "Your father wouldn't have liked what you did."

No. When I used to urge him to move Mom to a nursing home if caring for her became too hard on him, he said, "No wife of mine will live in a nursing home. Ever."

Dad, please oh please don't hate me for doing this. I hate myself enough.

I kept sheet music at Aunt Dora's. Through my forties during Buffalo visits, I played my parents' piano. My mother sat on the bench, singing. Songs from *The Fantasticks, Oklahoma,* and *My Fair Lady* were her favorites. My father sang and danced around the living room in his Bermuda shorts to "I'm Getting Married in the Morning" and "With a Little Bit of Luck," often grabbing Mom to join him. Stanley Holloway and company. The spirit was grand.

I played the piano at the nursing home. My mother did not sing anymore, but she knew the songs and enjoyed my playing. Until other residents gathered around. Then she'd get fidgety. One time when they started singing along, she said to me, "Let's go. I'm getting a headache. You're ruining my day."

I stopped playing. "Mom, this is *our* day." My voice quivered. She could still make me feel like shit.

Then I glanced down at her, at my white-haired mother in a wheelchair with a hearing aid in each ear, and her swollen ankles, with her Burdines flowered pocketbook on her lap. How sad she looked! How sad old age must be!

I wheeled her out of that sitting area, pausing to talk to her, to find out what might make the headache I'd given her go away. "How about we go watch *Oprah* or watch the other residents watch *Oprah*?" I said, rubbing my hand up and down her arm.

She smiled. My poor little mom.

In time, she blossomed. Relaxed. Except for a scowling night aide, Tonya, whom she called Lasagna, she called most of the staff members in her unit 'Marge,' the name of her big-hearted neighbor. Like Dolores in the Florida nursing home, Janeka, her doting home aide the previous year, and the waitress at the Pembroke Pines deli who used to give my parents brown paper bags of rolls to take home – I threw out eleven bags of rolls from the freezer after my father died – the new Marges showered her with attention.

"Let's leave this dump, Marge," she told her favorite

aide. "My daughter's crazy and I want to find something I don't have anymore."

"What?" the aide said.

"Max," said Mom.

Another Marge polished her nails with wild colors. A kitchen Marge gave her extra pudding. Wracked with guilt, I was grateful Mom found Marges.

And grateful, too, that I found an extracurricular activity in Buffalo. When the paperback of my book, *Writing from Personal Experience*, was published, I made an appointment with the events coordinator at the Jewish Community Center next door to the Weinberg Campus. I proposed offering a writing workshop on a weekend I'd be visiting.

She leafed through my book, shaking her head. "This is the Jewish Center. We only do events connected to Judaism. She handed me back my book. "This isn't a fit. What is Jewish here?"

"I have a lot of guilt," I said.

She scheduled a three-hour Sunday morning workshop eight weeks from our meeting so she'd have time to promote it in their bulletin and newsletter.

My twenty-nine attendees included: Aunt Dora, one of her Mah-Jongg ladies, two from her Canasta club, two cousins, friends of relatives, onetime classmates, and the ex-wife of my senior prom date.

The three hours flew. I gave several writing exercises. Everyone wrote. Everyone was engaged. Some read their work aloud and they offered insightful comments on each other's writing. I loved the energy. We had great "rappaport."

Afterwards, my cousin's friend from Toronto, who'd been writing for years, approached me with several questions. I mentioned one of my Camp Tamakwa counselors was from Toronto. "She was a real witch," I said. He asked me her name. I told him. "I've been married to that witch for thirty-two years," he said.

Among the things I learned at the JCC that Sunday morning: it's best not to gossip. If that was impossible, gossip only with Louise. She knew more and talked faster than anyone.

After my workshop, a short, nice-looking man, waiting outside my classroom in a designer sweat suit and about to use the center's gym, introduced himself. Alex Stamm, a Buffalo native. I recognized his name. His family owned a chain of supermarkets when I was growing up. They now belonged to him.

"I saw your name and workshop in the JCC bulletin and on today's schedule. That's cool you wrote a book," he said. He mentioned his father had lived at Weinberg before he died, and had heard my mother was there now. "I'd be happy to take you out if you could benefit from male company when you're in town."

I could. I gave Alex my Manhattan number and Aunt Dora's. He called me at Aunt Dora's two hours later and picked me up an hour after that. We went to Anderson's on Main Street, my choice.

The roast beef on kimmelweck with horseradish followed by chocolate frozen custard in a sugar cone, childhood favorites, almost made up for Alex's cracks. His last girlfriend "came from the wrong side of the tracks" and was an "utter embarrassment" at his country club picnic. My cousin, his onetime classmate with whom he sat on charity boards, did not have to look "so mousy." She had nothing but free time and money. And my Aunt Dora's sofa with "that shiny fabric" was not something he could sit on or "ever call classy."

Classy. That's what I might have called Alex when I first saw him at my workshop door.

I wondered if anxiety made him shoot off his mouth. First dates were so nerve-wracking. Perhaps he couldn't relax.

Giving him the benefit of the doubt, I asked him about himself, his interests and his work. Growing up, he learned the ropes of the business, doing assorted jobs, becoming a manager, and then little by little taking over. "Never having worked elsewhere crippled me," he said. "I'm a poor little rich boy with no clue who I am."

My journey and choices had been so different. I actually felt sorry for Alex.

We made a date to go on his boat in three weeks during my next visit. Not because I wanted the role of sympathetic social worker, but my guilt about 'parking my mother' so far from where I lived had gotten worse in recent months. I could use the company of new people. My Buffalo support team had dwindled.

Aunt Dora turned eighty. Walking into a nursing home depressed her. She saw my mother less and less. A cousin, another regular, got sick and stopped visiting. So did her family.

One by one the Marges left for jobs in other Weinberg units or elsewhere. My mother complained about the food, her stomach, bedtime, and Lasagna. Lasagna and her scowl were still there.

Arranging for Alex to pick me up at Weinberg would delight Mom. She'd think I was popular. He had that fine coat of polish. And giving someone a second chance seemed like a good idea. Particularly if that someone had a boat.

"You should have told me a man was coming," my mother said three weeks later when I introduced her to Alex. "I would have changed my clothes." She gave him a once-over, her eyes studying his face. "We shopped at your stores before we had Wegmans. No reason anymore. Wegmans is better."

Alex laughed, but seemed unable to show my mother any warmth. I bent down to tell her I'd be back later. In a very quiet voice she said, "Daddy won't like him. Better they don't meet."

I didn't want to leave with Alex. I wanted to stay with Mom.

Alex's twenty-two foot boat, a sloop he named *Sloopy*, was docked near the Peace Bridge. I thought about the Camp Tamakwa bus, which left from here, and about Crystal Beach where we had lakefront cottages. This setting, with the boats on the Niagara River, could not have been more romantic. Alex started the motor and got us out quickly. I stood next to him at the wheel.

"Want to steer?" he said, stepping aside, allowing me to take over, and getting close behind me. Too close.

I started steering. The nearness of a man who put me off on land, nauseated me on water. "Not now." *Not ever.* I gave him back his wheel.

When I was thirty-nine and dating the Hebrew calligrapher, who two thousand years ago might have been a catch, offered to take me to Paris for my fortieth birthday. Nothing came out of my mouth. I wanted to bolt.

Paris and boats were for lovers.

After a short, uncomfortable boat ride and a short, more uncomfortable car ride back to The Weinberg Campus, I was beside my mother on the sofa in the lounge.

"You don't look like you saw stars on that guy's boat," she said.

"No stars. I didn't like him."

She didn't chastise me for being too picky. "You'll figure it out," she said. "You always have."

I reached for her hand. We sat quietly watching the aides begin to wheel residents to the dining area for dinner. "Do you want to go eat now?" I asked.

"In a little while. What's my hurry?"

I gave her a hug. She flinched. "I'm just trying to get close to you, Mom," I said.

She looked at me in silence and then said, "You are?"

I nodded. "I like you and I love you."

Her shock, like my father's when I told him I loved him, choked me up.

"I love you and I like you, too," she said.

My parents found those words and physical displays of affection so difficult. They loved me, though. A lot.

We noticed Lasagna, sitting alone in a comfortable chair, in front of a television. Aides continued moving and helping residents to the dining area. She didn't budge.

"Lasagna doesn't like me," my mother said.

"Lasagna doesn't seem to like anyone, Mom."

My mother started fidgeting. "She's mean to me at bedtime."

On my way out, I spoke with the social worker.

The next afternoon, as I was saying goodbye to catch my plane back to New York, my mother asked, "Why can't I come with you?"

Her question reminded me of eight-year-old me forty-five years earlier stuck in the children's dining room at the Nevele Country Club and uncomfortable after one lunch. "Why can't I eat with you?" I pleaded with my parents.

I could. For the rest of that vacation, I sat between my mother and father in the main dining room.

I was not as good a parent to my eighty-five-year-old mother.

When Mom died several months later, the doctor wrote "heart attack" on the death certificate. They had to put something. Who knew?

At the nursing home the night before the funeral, when we picked up a pair of slacks and a sweater in which to bury Mom, Lasagna was on duty.

"Sorry about your mother," she said.

"How was she when you put her to bed her last night?" *She's mean to me at bedtime,* Mom had told me.

"Fine." Lasagna walked away.

I prayed my mother died of natural causes. Without harm or fear. I prayed, shall always pray, she found bags of rolls in heaven and angels she calls Marge.

Part Six

When One Door Closes . . .
Another Door Shuts

I'll call him Sheldon.

We went together for almost two years when he left me at the beginning of dinner, in the middle of Japonica, at the end of September, one week after my fifty-fifth birthday. On his way out, he stopped to speak to the hostess. Then he wove through the people waiting at the door and under

Japonica's awning, disappearing up University Place.

I finished our eel roll.

The waiter appeared at our small window table, now my small window table. He poured the last few drops of sake into my tiny gray cup.

I finished that too, and stared at his sweet young face. This was his first week at Japonica. It was my twenty-fifth year. If I didn't feel so awful, I would have welcomed the waiter, even discussed my favorite appetizers and makis, and told him I weaned my daughter here.

"Your nigiri sushi. I bring?" he said.

"I don't know yet," I told him.

"But your gentleman friend. He paid."

My gentleman friend! He always did the right thing in the world. He'd never stiff the Japanese.

"If you put our dinners in a bag, I'll take them home," I said.

Home. A big, empty apartment and my doorman's pitying smile. Earlier, he and Sheldon had been discussing the Knicks. When my marriage ended, I had to tell my parents and daughter. Now it was my building and restaurant staffs.

On the tablecloth next to Sheldon's half-eaten hijiki were several low sodium soy sauce spots. Moments before his departure, he accidently knocked over the bottle. A few drops splattered onto his yellow polo shirt an inch from the little mallet. He dabbed them with a wet napkin. When *that* didn't work, he put saliva on his index and third fingers and tried cleaning the shirt with his spit. He raged at his spots in the same tone he raged at me, unable to discriminate which was the worse screwer-upper. I took the high road and his hand without saliva. Sounding less like a woman scorned than a reassuring special education teacher, I delivered what were to be the last seven words of our relationship: "Low sodium soy sauce comes out, Sheldon."

Alone at the table, I stared out the window, looking up and down University Place again. No sign of Sheldon. Not on 12th Street either.

I knew early on we would break up one day. I didn't know when or how.

Years before, a psychologist I met on Fire Island, with whom I had a brief relationship, loved making observations. About me. On weekends by the ocean, he offered free therapy. One day, as we walked along the beach collecting seashells, he said, "You have a lot of guys running around inside of you."

Didn't we all have many people inside us fighting to direct traffic? Direct our lives? With Sheldon as with other men I tried to love, loneliness trumped passion and my wrong guys took the lead.

We started seeing each other when my mother was alive. In Buffalo at the nursing home during a weekend visit when he accompanied me, I asked Mom what she thought of him when he went to make a business call.

"What I think doesn't matter. You're the one who has to go for him and maybe eventually sleep with him, right?" she said.

"Right." I reached for her hand, cracking up. I wasn't

about to spill the details of my present or "eventual" sex life. It surprised me – though it shouldn't have – that Sheldon, a well-dressed CEO who looked like a card-carrying mother pleaser, did not seem to please mine. She had seen through Alex Stamm's fine coat of polish. She knew instinctively who was and wasn't a mensch.

I met Sheldon on a Friday evening at a restaurant across from Lincoln Center near the West Side Y where I would be attending a friend's reading from her new novel. I had walked uptown, had a half hour to kill, and sat down at the bar next to him. He wore a blue dress shirt and paisley tie tossed over his shoulder, was eating salmon and a salad and talking to the bartender with a familiarity that made me think he was a regular. I heard him say he was on his way to see *All About My Mother*. I had plans to see it the next day with Wendy. I jumped in, volunteering the information that I would be seeing the Almodovar movie too.

We chatted and bantered easily. His smarts were immediately apparent. He asked if I wanted to discuss the movie after the weekend. Giving my phone number to a stranger at a bar was a no-no even if the stranger liked Almodovar, looked like a respectable Jewish man, and seemed harmless. I asked for his business card. He gave it to me. I called him Monday at work.

On our first date at a cozy, upscale West Village restaurant, when the waiter served our dinners and he tossed his tie over his shoulder so he wouldn't spill on it, I was charmed. On Date # Two, when he told me he was not divorced, just separated, I was not. I shut down. I wanted an available partner, not a married man. He assumed I was too upset to order dessert. Nuh uh! I ordered a profiterole and ate it in silence. Then I bid him adieu and said, "Please don't call me again."

He did. At eight o'clock the next morning. After apologizing he asked what he would have to do to see me. I told him to hire a divorce lawyer *and* a therapist.

He did. We got together. I hung in, overlooking even worse news than his marital status: he was a Republican.

For a while, it worked. Or I made it work. With my mother in a nursing home in another city, I was consumed with guilt. Sheldon's presence soothed me. Distracted me. We went to plays and concerts. Every weekend, we tried new restaurants. Early on, we doubled with Louise and her husband.

"He's exactly how you described him," she said in the ladies room. "It's good you have a guy around."

A guy with a good mind, rooftop pool, Carnegie Hall subscription, kids and grandchildren, whom I adored, helped.

Helped, but didn't do it. The chemistry I had had with Robert – that glue my mother insisted a couple needs – was not there.

Did most women fake it – orgasms and everything else – to get what we were taught to want? SECURITY. Security plus two sides. Security and whatever came with.

As if security came from anything or anyone outside of ourselves.

Things went south when Sheldon got fired after mouthing off at his boss once too often. Shortly after that, he fired his divorce attorney, took back the invitation he had extended to his daughter's wedding, and got a job in Philadelphia, which he managed to keep a secret until he began to pack. Then he asked if I wanted to move there with him.

I didn't. For a month, he came in every weekend. He attended a wedding in New Jersey to which I had invited him. It was our first time dancing. Not a lot of fun.

We hung by a thread until ten minutes ago when he snapped over our hijiki and eel.

I glanced around Japonica's main room. How scary my friendly neighborhood restaurant suddenly looked! I managed to stand and put one foot in front of the other, getting myself to the restroom to brush my tousled hair which, unlike everything else, fell into place. The color in my face, like Sheldon, was gone. I left my blush at home, so I dotted my cheeks with lipstick, rubbing it in with my fingertips, and then applied it to my lips.

A young woman flossing over the other sink watched. "That shade's great. What is it?"

"Burt's Bees *Strength.* It's been discontinued." The woman flicked food particles into the mirror. "It looks pretty on you. Too bad everything good seems to get discontinued."

Everything bad does too.

Slowly and unsteadily, I walked back to my table, like a blindfolded Wendy on Captain Hook's gangplank. I felt invisible, too. No one eating sushi and sashimi here knew

I was alive.

The kitchen door swung open. I caught a whiff of teriyaki. When I was married, I used to make beef teriyaki for our three-couple dinner parties, if I didn't make fondue. For the two of us, I made simple, basic meals. My husband loved my meatloaf and beef stew. "If we ever split up, invite me for meatloaf and stew," he once said.

A small, brown paper shopping bag was on my window table. I glanced outside. The people waiting under Japonica's awning looked younger than people who had waited for tables last week. Everyone around me sat with at least one other person. I had two dinners for one. I started to stand with my dinners to go, but my body stuck to the chair. A tear fell.

"Here." The owner, in light blue silk pants and jacket, and a very severe short haircut, which Sheldon had told her was "most becoming," was standing next to my chair. She handed me a pile of napkins. "How long did your friend stay?"

"Fifteen minutes."

Sheldon's grand exit was 'just like that.' And it wasn't. Sudden departures are like overnight successes. They take time to build.

The owner fidgeted with her top button, her eyes darting around. She seemed anxious to check on her raw fish and on customers who had not been dumped. "No, I mean he has been eating here with you for a long time."

"Almost two years," I said, "but I've been a regular customer since you opened."

"I know." She put her hand on my shoulder. "Everything works out." She pointed to the bag. "I gave you extra wasabi and ginger." In a lower voice, she added, "Don't tell anyone, but I had the chef make you the deluxe."

Every time the phone rang, I folded my hands and prayed: *Let it be Sheldon. I regret whatever pain I inflicted. I'm sorry if I caused you to bolt. Come back. Please. I'd like to work it out.* I also wanted to say: *Go fuck yourself, you little dick. I hope you rot in hell.*

A week later he called, wanting to pick up his CDs, asking if I'd like to have dinner. I said no, but suggested he come up to the apartment for a glass of wine.

"Should we continue long distance?" he asked, sitting on the sofa.

I sat in a chair six feet from him. "Continue what?"

He chuckled. "Would you reconsider moving to Philly?"

"No." I would not have considered moving to Philadelphia, even if he had asked when he got the job offer and let me know he wanted to build a life, or something, with me.

I wanted that magic. Settling would not work. Although I did not have everything I wanted, I loved the life I created in New York.

So Sheldon took his CDs and a little part of me. Although most of the "guys running around inside of me" agreed the time had come to move on, it hurt. Endings never failed to hurt.

I sat in the tub. I drank more wine. I picked up the

picture I kept on the piano of Sheldon's two granddaughters jumping waves with me at the Jersey Shore. What fun I had holding their hands, babysitting, and reading William Steig's *Pete's a Pizza* before kissing them goodnight. These darling girls, their parents, and Sheldon enriched me.

I went about my life. I wrote. I read. I taught. I saw my friends. I played my piano. I played Wendy's pianos, the one in her apartment and the one at her country house. "What is that?" she asked one afternoon in the country as I was fiddling around with a melody.

I shrugged.

"It's nice." She opened the bench and took out a book of staff paper. "Write it down."

Wendy's father had been a composer. She liked writing melodies and lyrics and had a good ear. As I put the notes on paper, an idea for a musical came to her. A super one!

We took a course in writing for the musical theater at the New School. Separate and together, she and I wrote lyrics and melodies of six songs.

Then for many reasons, including work, a lack of confidence, and knowing we didn't have the chops, we stopped. But our collaboration had been a hoot and a half. Whenever we got together, we played and sang our songs.

I reached out to Pete. We had not spoken in a few years. I asked if he was interested in catching up over a weekend meal.

"I'm having a big party on Saturday."

"I guess you weren't planning on inviting me," I said.

"We haven't been in touch in ages. Sure. Come. Eight o'clock."

"Are you throwing it just like that or is it a special occasion?" I asked.

"I have a brain tumor," Pete said. His surgery was scheduled for Tuesday. He'd give me the details in person.

It was a potluck brain tumor party. I brought brownies with nuts.

Pete, heavier than when I had last seen him, did not wallow in self pity or seem even a little anxious. I knew a few of his friends. We remarked on his good spirits and clinked glasses together, toasting him.

Pete had a piano, but no sheet music. I sat down and played the songs I knew: "Over the Rainbow," "What's the Use of Wondering" from *Carousel*, and "Both Sides Now."

Something's lost and something's gained in living every day.

First our parents. Now our friends. So what's to be gained from all our losses and illnesses? Dear Joni, what's to be gained?

I told Pete I would help him through this ordeal. I would be there in whatever ways I could.

On Tuesday, I visited him at Mt. Sinai and was told his surgery went well. On Thursday, when I got to the hospital, he had been moved to intensive care. Something happened late Wednesday. They found water in his brain.

Pete had a second operation, spent a week in rehab, and went home with a shunt and a live-in aide.

He stopped working. His weight soared. He took all kinds of medication and was more than a tad doped up.

His other friends, who visited at first, stopped coming around. Being company for Pete was company for me. It beat my own pity party.

One Friday, I called to tell him I would bring over Chinese food for him, his aide, and me. He said he felt strong enough and wished to go to a restaurant. When I arrived, we were alone.

"I gave Keisha the night off," Pete said.

Using his cane and holding onto me, he walked slowly – very slowly – to a restaurant a block from his apartment. Moving, eating, and talking clearly tired him out.

"Maybe call Keisha so she can meet us here and help me walk you home," I said.

"I told you Keisha's off tonight." He sounded indignant, as if I missed or hadn't heard something important. "She'll be back tomorrow."

"But you can't stay alone," I said.

Pete had the energy to smile. "I want to experiment."

"With what?" Oy!

"You." His smile widened. "I want to see if I'm able to . . . you know . . . do it."

"Do it? I offered to bring over Chinese food. I don't remember volunteering to be your guinea pig." *And night nurse, sleep-over concubine, medicine giver, and possible emergency doctor.*

Years earlier, when we dated, I accepted his discounting me and not seeing us as a "we." I knew what we were and weren't. But what he asked of me now with a shunt in his head, water in his brain, a tumor that might or might not be all out, and a belly that protruded onto the table showed less sensitivity and more chutzpah than I could handle.

I counted to three. "Pete, we're friends. We decided a while back we do friendship well. Thinking about having sex with me tonight is a little unrealistic. Actually, it's bananas." I continued speaking softly, staying in control. "Did you think to ask if it was something I might consider?"

Pete did not answer.

Men.

I went on. "Please call Keisha."

"She told me not to unless I really need her."

Managing to continue keeping my voice low, I said, "Pete, you *really* need her."

Pete sulked. On what felt like a turtle crawl to his apartment, he remained silent. I waited until Keisha showed up and said goodbye.

After that night, whenever I called, Pete was either monosyllabic or didn't come to the phone. He developed further complications and got a new live-in aide. I did not ask if he gave her nights off or found willing guinea pigs.

I continued checking in with Pete for health updates. By telephone.

I decided to throw a Chanukah party and told the thirty-three people I invited to bring a twenty-dollar present for the grab bag. Marilyn, the caterer I hired, invited me over beforehand to sample chicken wings in different sauces, cheeses, dips, and wines. Wendy accompanied me. Although I worried as I had since childhood that no one would come to my party, getting ready for it helped ward off the holiday blues.

Emily, living on the Upper East Side, called Sunday morning of the party to see what she could do. If no one else showed up, she and I could light the menorah – the "menormah" she called it as a little girl – and eat.

She arrived first. Then came Wendy and her husband with a coat rack followed by my next-door neighbor with meatballs. Other guests began arriving, many with their children. My upstairs neighbors brought a guy. A single, unkempt, unsmiling, uncommunicative guy. For me.

He sat like a lump near the coat rack. I ushered him over to a comfortable chair and introduced him around. He didn't want to talk to the other guests or to me. I made him a huge plate of food.

My neighbors, who brought him, had another party. They left early, taking presents from the grab bag. And fortunately the guy.

The rest of the evening turned out great. I loved having people of different ages from different places in my life at my apartment eating, talking, and laughing. A writer friend with his wife and grandson lit the menorah and said the blessing over it together.

My favorite part: excusing myself for ten minutes and going into my bedroom with my daughter where we gossiped and exchanged gifts.

I had not seen my neighbor, Diana, for a while. Several

times before the Chanukah party, I knocked on her door to invite her. Would she have come? I wondered if she had ever lit a menorah, seen a menorah, eaten potato latkes, or knew what a latke was.

One night very late, I took the garbage to the incinerator room wearing a new black nightgown under my ski jacket. Diana there without make-up and in jeans and a sweatshirt – a new look for her – was throwing out newspapers, a suitcase, and a few empty cardboard cartons.

"Hello stranger," I said. "I thought you might have moved."

"I've been in Europe, mostly in London. But I am moving." She smiled. "To California. I met someone."

Diana's met many someones. I had no idea what to say. Finally I asked, "Do you want to tell me more?"

She smiled again. "I'm getting married. My fiancé lives in La Jolla. His house is too small for us both. We just closed on a huge one right on the water."

"Wow! Diana, that's really great." Had her fiancé been a customer? Did they meet on her job? Did he know what kind of work she did? Did he love that? Hate it? Care? "I bet he's fabulous."

"And handsome." Her smile widened. "We're heading back to London for five days next week. He travels a lot."

"What does he do?"

"He's in business."

I didn't ask what kind.

Diana's eyes went to the plunging neckline of my nightgown. "You got company?"

I shook my head. "I'm not seeing anyone."

"What happened to that last guy?"

"It's over. He wanted to get back together after we split up. Lately, I've thought about reconsidering."

She shook her head. "No. Don't. If it wasn't right the first time, why would it be now?" She looked me up and down. "When you start seeing someone again . . . and you will . . . wear that nightgown. It's ooh la la."

"Thanks. I actually bought this for myself."

"Good. Buy more. You don't want to wear the same one all the time."

I laughed. "Anything else?"

"When someone you like comes over, put on a little music. Pour him a glass of wine. Don't tell him your problems."

"That wouldn't be so real."

"Take it from me: reality doesn't pull 'em in."

Saturday, on our walk along the Hudson River, I told Wendy about Diana. "Two more people are going into the Ark and neither one is me."

"Getting married and moving into a house together aren't such hard things to do," Wendy said. "I've seen Diana. She not that much younger than we are. Old for her line of work. Was he a client?"

"I don't know."

Wendy walked at her usual rapid clip. Her long legs made for easy strides. I practically sprinted to keep up. We had gotten as far as Stuyvesant High School today. Some days we walked past the Holocaust Museum to the tip of

Manhattan. Now we headed back up, crossed Christopher Street, and went to Elephant and Castle for lunch.

I continued on about Diana and her fiancé. "What about love?" I asked.

"What about it? You always ask if people love each other. Who knows? Who knows what love is, anyway? People get and stay married for a lot of reasons."

"Well, I hope Diana loves him and he loves her."

Wendy said, "Me too."

Midway through lunch, she said, "So, I've got some news, too." A pause. "We're retiring. Our apartment's on the market."

I put down my fork. "You're kidding, right?"

"I'm not. We're moving to the country house. We can't keep two places."

"How come you're just getting around to telling me now?"

Wendy looked down. "I wasn't sure how to do this. The whole thing's been stressing me out."

The waiter came by and asked if we were done. Wendy nodded. I did, too. Not finishing my food was a rare occurrence for me.

"Listen, none of this was my idea," Wendy said. "It's been really depressing me. I don't want to move to the country."

"I don't want you to go."

"We haven't left yet," she said. "It's gonna take a while to sell the apartment."

It took no time at all. The real estate agent found a buyer immediately. Wendy made plans to move, to leave. Since our children were little, she'd been part of my everyday life. "It's worse than a death," I told her.

"You'll come and visit whenever you want. Nothing's gonna change."

Right.

My second-floor apartment faced the street. The morning of the move, I watched the movers park the van. In the elevator up to Wendy's, my stomach dropped to my knees. Twenty years of going there for meals, food, love, comfort, and friendship were about to end.

Wendy, her husband, and I watched the movers carry out cartons, furniture, and artwork. Watched the apartment empty out.

"You'll visit soon," her husband said, hugging me goodbye. "And I'll be coming to the city to see the eye doctor in a few weeks. I'll make sure Wendy drives in with me."

He went down to the van. I started to cry.

"What am I gonna do without you?" I asked Wendy.

"Think of it as a positive move. I'm creating a space for you to find someone. Someone great."

"Like anyone could ever replace you."

"He'll be better," she said.

"Than you?"

Time to go. We got into the elevator. When it opened at the lobby, we hugged. "I'll miss you," she said, in tears. "I love you. We'll speak. We'll visit. We're family."

Why did the cheese have to move?

Emily and I met at the Kips Bay Movie Theater the Sunday afternoon after *Match Point* opened. Arriving forty-five minutes before its starting time, we were the second ones in the ticket holders' line. She had a stress fracture and wore a boot cast on her left leg.

"Nice of you to meet me in your condition," I said.

"You probably wouldn't enjoy seeing a Woody Allen movie alone."

"Probably not. I'm happy I'm seeing it with you, though," I said. "This one's not supposed to be enjoyable exactly."

We discussed what we heard about *Match Point,* that it was grim, not funny. I looked down at her cast. "Are you going to stop running now?" I had asked her the same question when she had her last stress fracture.

"Until the doctor says I'm good to go," she said. Same answer, too.

A longtime Woody Allen fan, I tried to see his movies the week they opened, feeling about them, even the lesser ones, the way he did about sex. Even when it's bad, it's good. And better than most movies around.

Match Point was unsettling. Afterwards at Patsy's on Third Avenue, over a pizza with pepperoni and a Sicilian Salad we split, we discussed people getting away with murder and men disposing of women when they no longer met their needs.

As we were about to part, she said, "This worked out well today. The guy I'm seeing isn't a big Woody Allen fan."

Guy? "I didn't know you were seeing anyone." I hadn't

known Wendy was moving either until she was practically out the door.

A few days after Sheldon walked out of Japonica, I bumped into a woman I knew. She asked about Sheldon. After quietly listening to a long, detailed version of the break-up, she said, "I've got to go call my brother. Our father died yesterday. We have to arrange the funeral."

"How come you waited to tell me your father died?" I asked her.

"Your story's more interesting. Besides I'm a WASP."

But why did Emily and Wendy wait to share their news? Were they sparing me? Afraid I'd feel abandoned?

"Anything you want to tell me about your new guy?" I asked.

"Not really. We have a lot of fun when we're together. He's great." She blushed.

It WAS serious.

She went on, "We see each other every few weekends. He lived here but just got a job in LA and he's living in Santa Monica on the beach."

"Is he planning on moving back?"

She shrugged.

Oh well.

Alice, an instructor, with whom I occasionally had coffee or lunch, asked if I wanted to meet her smart, lovely, divorced friend, Charlie, a documentary film producer. She was sure we would hit it off.

Why not?

A week went by. Charlie didn't call. Alice did. "My friend won't be available after all."

"Why? What did you tell him about me?"

"Nothing," she said. "He died."

"Where is he buried?" I asked.

"A cemetery near his family's summer house in the Adirondacks."

"That's too far away," I told her.

Maybe not. After so many years with so many guys, who were not all there or "there" but borderline reptilian, why would "not breathing" in the Adirondack Mountains be any more unavailable?

One afternoon when I phoned home from The Writers Room, where I worked most days, I heard a message from Elliot. Something terrible happened. Please call.

Irene was sick. It started with flu-like symptoms. When she didn't get better, she went to the doctor. It turned out to be a weird strand of pancreatic cancer. "The doctor said it's incurable," Elliot said.

I wanted to fly out to Portland. Elliot said no. Irene was too exhausted, in bed all the time, and in pain. In between, they sought out specialists, trying to find answers and cures, and dealing with family: their kids, her parents, and a new granddaughter. A visit would be too much.

It hadn't occurred to me the last several Sundays when I didn't hear from her that something might be wrong. I thought that they had gone to their Black Butte house or were helping with the baby. Or that Irene, a divorce attorney, had a slew of new cases.

Irene and I were only fifty-nine.

"Does she know how sick she is?" I asked Elliot.

"Yes." He told me their one-month-old granddaughter napped in their bedroom one day and that Irene felt too sick to get up and hold her. "I'll never play with her," she said. "I'm not going to see this baby grow up."

The third time I called, Elliot put Irene on. I could not believe how weak she sounded.

"I'm so sorry, Irene. I'm thinking of you all the time. I wish I could do something for you," I said.

"Thank you, Nancy. Shit happens. I had a great life. You had a lot to do with that."

We spoke several more times in the next six weeks. She had so little energy. I filled the space with memories, trying to keep it light. "When I told you that you looked like a giraffe and you laughed, I knew we'd be great friends."

I reminded her of the sweaters with reindeer on the front Elliot wore when they met and how he forgot to wash his hair. "You pinned little notes on the reindeer to remind him to do so."

At the bridesmaids' luncheon Irene threw the day before her daughter's wedding, I was the only friend she invited. After eating, I showed the young women around her huge house, up one staircase and down the other, pretending to be a tour guide. Then Irene showed them pictures of the two of us at her 1968 wedding. "There's Little

Nancy, my maid of honor, in the green velvet dress," she said. "I'm the giraffe in white lace."

I let her know how much she meant to me. "You were the best roommate in the world, Irene."

"Thank you, Nancy. You were such a slob."

I was Oscar. Irene was Felix. On her side, no clothing or notebooks were scattered about. No make-up or brushes were on her dresser top. On my side, everything was thrown around. Nothing had a place.

"I'm still Oscar," I told her.

One night her son phoned. Irene was in a hospice. "Mom wants to say good-bye to you." He put Irene on.

"You've been an amazing friend," I told her.

"You have, too. Thank you for Elliot." She sounded so tired. So weak. "I'm glad you were in my life. You made it fun."

"What can I do for you, Irene?" This was the hardest conversation I ever had.

"Check in on Elliot. He'll probably be lost." A pause, then, "Take care of Little Nancy."

Two weeks after Irene died I got severe chest pains sitting at my computer at The Writers Room. I went by cab to my doctor's office and saw his associate, a cardiologist. "I think I might be having a heart attack."

After giving me a stress test and an EKG, he said, "You're not. What's been going on in your life?"

"One of my best friends died."

"That can do it. Try to take it easy."

"Sure." Taking it easy, I could manage. Taking care of Little Nancy was something else.

"You have a lot of good years left," the doctor said.

Good years? Do we ever know?

On the bookcase next to my writing desk, I have a silver-framed, five-by-seven-inch black and white photo of Irene laughing. On Sunday nights between eight and nine, the time she used to call, I stand in front of it and talk to her as I do each morning before I sit down at my desk. I look at her laughing face and I smile. Then I start with "Hello Giraffe."

As a child, saying it funny became my tool, and kept my sadness at bay. Laughing at Mom's absence and at all I thought was wrong with me covered my tender spots, became My Way.

Funny did not work when Irene died.

A friend was gone and I was approaching sixty. She experienced the kind of love I hadn't. Will I miss the boat? Sixty! At sixty, my parents rushed to early bird dinners and spent the rest of the night discussing what and where they would eat the next day. I still watched men I hardly knew pick our wine and their teeth.

Teeth. I decided to reach out to my dentist. Dr. D got divorced five years before when I got my second inlay. For two decades, our relationship had been primarily about teeth. Mine. Every so often, when neither his fingers nor instruments were in my mouth, we conversed about New York, music, books, and our kids. I enjoyed talking with him. I made an appointment for my regular check-up before I was due.

"I can't go through with it," I said to Wendy. "How do I tell him I want to get beyond rinsing and spitting?"

"Wear a black tank top," she said. "That'll do it."

On the phone, Louise reminded me of Billy Miller, the first boy to send me a valentine. From seventh grade on, he had pretty girlfriends. At our twentieth high school reunion, Billy asked me – *me* – to dance the first slow one. Not in high school, before, or after had I ever danced with him. I asked if he remembered sending me a valentine. He nodded.

"I slept with it under my pillow," I said. "I had such a crush on you."

"You should have told me. I had one on you, too."

As we danced cheek to cheek, I wondered what might have happened had I shared my feelings back then. Would Billy and I have gone together through high school? To the senior prom? To the altar? We probably weren't destined to build a life together, but that first slow dance got me thinking about other missed opportunities, the what ifs, and the many other Billy Millers with whom I did not connect out of fear. Fear. The primary reason we don't move off the dime.

I wore a black tank top and my invisible Open for Business sign to Dr. D's office. The hygienist remained in the room talking to him when he finished looking in my mouth. I asked her if she could step out. I looked up at Dr. D. "I hope I'm not crossing a line being your patient, but I would like to have dinner with you if you are interested."

He stared at me impassively for what felt like an eternity. I had no idea if he was stunned. Touched. Flattered. Put off. In a quandary about what to do. Or nauseated. "Thank you," he finally said. "I have your number."

Dr. D did not call me. At my next appointment, he said nothing. I found out from the receptionist he had a girlfriend. "For a long time," she said. "She comes to our Christmas lunch. What a head-turner. And really sweet, too."

Dr. D retired, not because I hit on him. A new dentist dealt with my teeth, a periodontist with my receding gums. I wanted nothing more from my teeth men.

I gave it a shot with Dr. D. Took a risk. The only thing more terrifying: never having tried.

Part Seven

To My Rightstein

One Sunday, at age fifty-nine, my blues hit me hard at my friend Rita's sixtieth surprise birthday brunch. I'd known Rita since our twenties when I wrote reviews of Off-Off Broadway plays for a local newspaper. She was the photo editor. We'd go out for lunch, to dinner and the theater with our husbands, and to each other's apartments to parties.

I arrived early at the brunch with My Ride, another divorced friend of Rita's, who had a small car, a big mouth, and lactose intolerance. From lower Manhattan to The River Café in Brooklyn Heights, she shared the details of her symptoms and the treatment, stopping only when she glanced my way and said, "You know, you could use a little collagen."

At the party, I made small, *very* small talk at the buffet table, grateful not to be person number nine or number eleven at a sit-down meal with four or five couples, who got up to foxtrot and cha-cha while I sat alone with my fake smile. Here I could move around, mingle.

I was a good mingler. I knew many of Rita's other seventy-some closest people and chatted them up over the white fish salad and lox.

"Do you think she was really surprised?" I asked Madeline, another divorced friend.

"C'mon," Madeline said. "Knowing Rita, she probably had some idea."

"Probably." Did we *know* Rita?

Did we ever know other people? Or do we see Their Representatives? I showed up most places with My Representative: Perky, Perky Nancy. The part I chose to show.

After hearing about Madeline's lazy eye and lazy son, I moved along to Barb and Al, a longtime married couple who worked together in their optical store. I knew from Rita that Barbara had plastic surgery and that Al cheated on her.

"It's great you two can be together all day and all night,"

I said. "What's the secret?"

Al smiled. "I'm out a lot, screwing around." He put his arm around Barb.

I didn't know Barb knew. Or that Al discussed his cheating in her presence.

Barb nodded. "His last honey's our customer." Neither reacting nor smiling, although maybe she was, but who could tell with most of her face not moving, she spoke in the same matter-of-fact way that she mentioned they would be stopping at the Brooklyn Costco after the party and I was welcome to join them, treating her husband's philandering with more nonchalance than I did. Or could.

When he disappeared to refill his glass, I said to Barb, "You give Al a lot of rope."

She shrugged. "Al's always fucked around." She chuckled. "He fucked around on our honeymoon." A pause. "I'm not going anywhere."

My Ride, who knew Barb, joined us. Al returned and put his arm around his cuckolded wife. The conversation returned to Costco. I had never been there and had no desire to go. Then I glanced at my lactose intolerant driver. To Costco or trapped in the car again with her?

Two waiters in white chef hats wheeled in an enormous, white-frosted sheet cake. Rita, flanked by her husband, son, daughter-in-law, grandson, and her brother and sister-in-law, looked around the room beaming.

I sang "Happy Birthday" flanked by The Couple and My Ride.

As Rita made the first cut and wish, my Representative

and smile disappeared. I did, too, into the ladies room and into a stall. How did I get to be almost sixty without a partner? Without the love of a good man?

On my tombstone, will it say: Here lies Perky Nancy?

What about at the funeral service? Will someone say she prepared the face to meet the faces and worked whatever room she endured?

A woman came into the restroom and peed in the toilet on my left. Another had gas on my right. The one in the middle was the green kangaroo. How should a kangaroo proceed?

I heard people saying goodbye. Shall I put on my smile and tell the hosts and birthday girl what I should: "It was a lovely party. Thank you for inviting me. I had a wonderful time." My mother told me to say that when she drove me to my first birthday party. I did. I've been saying some version of that to my hosts for a half a century since then.

Ma, you learned me well.

My choices now? To Costco with The Couple? Or a ride home with My Ride? Shall I freak out in a massive store or endure another two-borough monologue from a bore?

Rhett, oh Rhett, what's to become of me? Like Scarlett without the seventeen-inch waist and Tara, was I destined to end up alone? My Ride had it wrong at the stop light on the way to this event. I could use a whole lot more than collagen. How would I get home?

I took Emily to Union Square Café for her thirtieth birthday. When she picked me up at the apartment, she got her beach cover-up and other summer clothes she had not taken when she moved. Tomorrow she'd be heading to Santa Monica to celebrate with her boyfriend, Teddy.

"What's Teddy like?" I asked. They had been seeing each other every few weeks for a while now.

I assumed she was about to rattle off the four-item checklist with which she described her last boyfriend: he's smart, he's kind, he's handsome, and he's funny.

No. "He gets me," she said. Her eyes sparkled. She returned to her menu.

WOO HOO! Maternal happiness knows no bounds. If one woman in the family could have a happy relationship, let it be the daughter.

Glancing up, she said, "What else do you want to know, Mom?"

"I want to know if we should share a couple of appetizers before our entrees or just order our own."

He gets her. What else did I have to know?

The next weekend Teddy came to New York, the three of us had a drink at Blue Water Grill on Saturday evening before they headed to dinner. When we first sat down, he seemed a little nervous. Good! Meeting me mattered.

He spoke about his job, his apartment across the street from the beach, which he loved, and his twin brother's upcoming wedding. Emily described the dress she bought for it — long, red, sleeveless, scooped-neck, simple. It sounded elegant. "Like the kind of dress that can take you anywhere," my mother would have said. Yes. Emily had style. Taste. Class.

Teddy talked about his job. The three of us discussed restaurants and books. I wondered how much his twin resembled him and what his fiancé was like. Emily had been invited to another family event the same day as their wedding and would not be attending it. She must be serious about this guy.

I hoped so.

Whether he got Emily or not, I could not tell in the half hour we spent together, but he sure seemed to adore her and, in addition to the four checklist items, he was very sweet.

On parting, he called me Mrs. Kelton. I told him Nancy would be fine. He shook his head. "I can't," he said. "How's Mrs. K?"

I wondered if his brother had the same smile. Teddy's lit up Manhattan.

My empty nest felt too empty. I had too many rooms. Not many people in Manhattan could say that they have too many rooms.

I considered renting out my daughter's. It didn't look as if she'd be back. My Grandma Davidoff had taken in boarders, all single and widowed men from the temple. She needed money, my father said. What about company? Maybe Grandma needed another human in her house, too?

I did not want a boarder of any sex or age sleeping in the next room. Who needed a stranger in the apartment?

I was strange enough.

I needed a paint job.

Not me. My living room, alcove, and kitchen. I decided to go yellow.

Finding the right shades – bright for the kitchen, subtle for the rest but not so subtle that it would be mistaken for off-white – required daily early morning trips to the paint store for sample jars and chips of lemon sorbet, lemon drops, lemon soufflé, little dipper, lightning bolt, wildflowers, good morning sunshine, pale straw, golden straw, old straw hat, and canary yellow.

For weeks, I went steady with Benjamin Moore.

Over lunch at Jackson Hole one day, I showed Louise the chips. She pointed to the two she liked most. "A decorator would do a better job saying what's right for you. Maybe you should hire one."

Maybe not. When my marriage ended, I hired a decorator. Entering my living room, he said, "Get rid of the bookcase and the books. They don't belong in here." I wrote the decorator a check for his time and got rid of him. He didn't belong in my living room.

For my kitchen now, I decided on good morning sunshine, for the living room and for the alcove, pale straw. The contractor said the job would take two to three weeks. With unforeseen cracks, bubbles, and other "issues" on the walls and ceiling requiring extra scraping and spackling, his painters and their drop cloths were in my apartment for seven.

When they left, I sat alone in my living room, staring

at my new yellow walls, hating them, and crying. I called Wendy. "Please come in. The living room is hideous. You'd never know it was yellow."

She arrived Friday afternoon with an overnight bag. "The color's perfect," she said walking around. "You're too close to really see it and too used to what you had. We need to feng shui."

Wendy and I got rid of my clutter, an old ripped recliner, and a broken end table. She bought me candlesticks at ABC Carpet. I took her to Japonica for dinner. I gave her my room and, since there was no longer a bed in the second bedroom, I put sheets on the living room sofa for me.

"We can both sleep in your bed," she said, "if you promise not to try anything funny." Wendy was kidding, I think.

"No promises. The sofa's fine."

Saturday morning when I woke up, she was scrubbing my kitchen floor. "Why are you doing that?" I asked.

"It needs it and you know I like cleaning," she said. About *that,* she definitely wasn't kidding.

We shopped. She helped me pick out blinds for the living room and alcove windows, an upholstered chair, two posters, three decorative pillows for the sofa, and a bookcase. The bookcase needed assembling.

On Sunday morning at seven-thirty, Claudio, the building handyman, came up and assembled it with Wendy. Then we all put my books on the shelves, hung up the posters, and rearranged furniture.

"It's like a different apartment," Claudio said.

Wendy walked around, nodding. "It's warm. Very gracious. Having no clutter helps. Promise me you'll keep it neat."

"You can do an inspection visit and clean up my next mess."

"Don't make one," she said. Then to Claudio now heading to the door, "You're sure going to be missed." She wished him luck.

Claudio worked in the building before either Wendy or I moved in. The tenants loved him, counted on him. He was about to retire.

"Thanks," he said. He put up his hands, shaking his head, as he always did when I tried to tip him.

"Your leaving's harder on me than Wendy's," I said. For thirty years, whenever a sink, toilet, radiator, and anything building-related or not needed fixing or assembling, Claudio came right up if he could, did the job, and refused to take a cent.

That evening, after Wendy left, I sat down at the piano in my freshly painted living room and played "For All We Know," "Are You Lonesome Tonight?" and "People Will Say We're in Love" from *Oklahoma*. My mother loved those songs. When I visited, as soon as she heard me play the first notes, she'd rush into the room, sit beside me on the bench, and sing. That had been my favorite part of Buffalo visits from college on, and among my favorite parts of "us."

When I finished those three songs now, I opened my *South Pacific* book and played "This Nearly Was Mine."

Shit! My apartment felt empty again.

When Robert proposed to me, he used his freshly wall-papered bathroom as a case for our building a life together. "It would have more fun picking out the paper with you and making this our bathroom, rather than having you over to admire it."

I got *that* now.

My A-team was moving on.

On Christmas Eve, my favorite member got engaged. Emily called to announce that Teddy proposed in front of the Connecticut church where his mother and father had gotten married. Teddy's parents were both deceased. How I wished I could pick up the phone and call them. How I wished we could plan to meet. We'd talk about the wonderful choices both our children made.

My maternal happiness and new yellow walls depressed me. During my routine physical the following week, I asked my longtime internist for antidepressants.

"I don't see you as a candidate. Why do you want antidepressants?"

"I'm lonely. I want a partner. A deep connection."

"Go on J-Date for a deep connection, not meds." His sister-in-law met her husband on J-date. "And she's about your age," he said.

At my next gynecological check-up, I asked Dr. Number Two for antidepressants. Getting the right one and the right dose might take time, she explained. Wasn't I too busy? "Why do think you need them, anyway?" she asked.

"I'd like to meet someone."

"Antidepressants won't get you the someone," she said. "Try J-Date."

Huh? Were my longtime doctors in cahoots? Getting advanced training from a matchmaker?

I shook my head. "I've tried the personals. Too hazardous." I told her about Mitch with his rage and Hank with the stent.

She laughed. "Several of my patients found guys on-line without stents on their testicles. Treat it as a job. Stay with it. Shop. Weed out the flotsam and jetsam."

I've been weeding out flotsam and jetsam my entire life. Had I looked with only one eye? What would happen if I used two?

I followed my doctors' orders. After posting a profile and picture I actually liked, I put on cute outfits and a cute face, and met enough guys to form several minyans, telling myself "you never know," even though you do.

Some men I met lied. One, who wrote "divorced" as his marital status told me over dinner, and only after I asked, that he couldn't see me on weekends, holidays, and evenings: he would be with his wife. "I assumed we were on the same wavelength," he said. "I thought you were also looking for a nooner."

A nooner!

Another man lied about his age. In his profile, Ronald

wrote he was "close to fifty-nine." He was closer to eighty-five at the café. Already at a table when I arrived, Ron was lining up five vials of pills.

I ordered a Bloody Mary. Ron ordered club soda. He pointed to two of his vials. "No alcohol with these. My doctor keeps changing my medication. Alcohol with some prescriptions spells disaster, if you know what I mean. "

I didn't. My doctors prescribed J-Date, not meds.

Ron continued. "I've got to stay healthy. My son's throwing himself a dinner dance next month for his fiftieth birthday."

Hmm. "Fifty! Amazing! So did your son learn to dance at your bar mitzvah?"

Ron looked into my eyes. "What are you saying?"

"You wrote you were close to fifty-nine."

"Oh." Ron winked. At least I think he winked. "So I stretched it a little. I wanted to meet an attractive younger woman. Would you have gone out with me if you knew my real age?"

"Maybe." An older man I could handle. Dinner with Leonard Cohen or Philip Roth might be great. So would meeting a less brilliant, less engaging older man who brought something a tad more interesting to the table than vials of pills and a lie.

I finished my salad, doing what I thought I should do, keeping the conversation light. "I like the dressing here," I said.

"Can we do this again, Nancy?"

A flat-out no might have insulted Ron. "I'm very busy

the next few weeks. Maybe after that."

I finished my grilled chicken and brown rice.

"How about we at least give it a whirl at my son's dinner dance?" Ron said.

"We'll see," I said, rather than *Liar, liar, pants on fire.* I already saw. I headed out. Ron did too. Only slower.

I went out with a divorced man who entertained me with stories about his "whore of an ex-wife." She took rich lovers and wanted no part of him after his company went under.

Then there was a prosperous businessman who found his purpose through wheeling and dealing and investing and scheming. Over our cold antipasto appetizer, he gazed into my eyes and said, "I worry I may have lost my soul. Maybe you can help."

I told him to look elsewhere for his missing soul. It was not inside of me.

Next was the sixties man, who in the twenty-first century, spent a lot of time saying "Yo" and "Far out." He baked a hundred to two hundred loaves of bread each week for a living, yet never got his hands dirty in a committed relationship. Only in dough.

Next I reached out to a widower. A geographically desirable widower who lived on 25th Street, nine blocks from my apartment. In his profile he wrote, "My super, solid forty-year marriage ended with my wife's death five years ago. I am ready and eager to commit again."

Perfect! Unlike some angry, divorced men, there'd be

no venting about his ex. And unlike the bread-baker, he could commit. With me, he could commit without taking a bus.

We met for brunch at Elephant and Castle. My regular spot with Wendy.

I ordered a spinach omelet. The geographically desirable widower ordered eggs Florentine. His next words after "eggs Florentine" were, "Helen would have ordered eggs Benedict. She always got eggs Benedict. Wanna know why?"

I didn't. He went on anyway. "Helen loved Canadian bacon. If a restaurant had eggs Benedict on the menu, there was no question she'd order it."

Our coffees arrived. "Helen didn't drink coffee, but she loved tea and brewed her own," he said. "Everyone who tasted Helen's teas marveled. Everyone loved Helen's blueberry muffins. And her sour cream coffee cake. No one's muffins and coffee cake came close."

I never missed Wendy as much as I did now.

When our food came, the widower said, "No one made English Muffins like Helen did."

"English Muffins from scratch?" I asked. "What happened to Thomas?"

The corners of his mouth turned up into a smile, but that immediately disappeared.

"Helen knew how to toast them. They came out just right."

"Wow!" I wanted Helen to be my wife. "Have you had any relationships with other women since Helen died?"

"Two. The first only lasted a month, the second over a

year. The first woman said I didn't seem ready to be with
anyone else, because I talked nonstop about Helen."

"Really?"

For the first time since we sat down, the widower
laughed. "I guess I still do that a little."

I nodded. "A little, but you must have toned down
with the second woman. A year's a long time."

He smiled. "I shut up with her. She gave great head."
He laughed again. "It was amazing. I didn't know oral sex
could be so amazing. Helen never gave great blow jobs. She
didn't like doing that." He looked at me for a few seconds,
remembering I was there. "Don't get me wrong. I didn't
mind. It just wasn't Helen's thing." Another pause and
in a lower voice, he added, "I felt guilty having such fun
with this woman. I became impotent." He started to cry.
He used his napkin to wipe his eyes and blow his nose. "I
shouldn't have had so much fun. It was like I cheated on
Helen."

What to say? What to do? I flagged our waiter and got
clean napkins. "Here," I said.

A nicer, more mature woman might have been empa-
thetic. I was not that nice. Or mature. What's more, I had
not found the widower attractive even before his dead wife
joined us.

And, had I thought he and I might go somewhere,
where would "our somewhere" be? Would I have to keep
my mouth shut except for use on him?

When it seemed as if he finished sniffling, he said, "Do
you think Helen would mind?"

Oh boy! "Mind?"

"That I had fabulous oral sex with another woman?"

"I'm sure she would have been thrilled for you," I said, not: *let's ask her.* How good I had gotten at singing for my supper. When could I stop singing and just eat? "Listen," I said. "I have enough issues to work on in therapy without feeling erased on a date." I finished my spinach omelet. I finished my home fries, too.

"I'm sorry, Nancy. Like I said, you're not the first person who told me I carried on about Helen."

I bet I was the first person to hear that Helen gave lousy head.

My mother used to tell me to give men second chances and the benefit of the doubt. I chastised myself for making snap judgments and not cutting people slack.

But for much of my life and with too many people, I've wasted a helluva lot of time. At sixty, I had no desire or time to be diminished or uncomfortable. My gut spoke louder than my mother now. I was getting the hang of "Next."

Next. A younger man emailed me, delighted I taught writing. Tolstoy, I'll call him, spared me his rage, meds, lies, and post-marital delight in blow jobs. Excellent!

He did not spare me his memoir-in-progress. "I'll bring it when we meet so you can read and critique it."

"Please don't. I only read manuscripts of the seventy-five students in my four classes."

In my twenties, I noticed a strange-looking growth on my arm and called a dermatologist acquaintance at home to discuss it. "Discussing warts at night nauseates me," he said. After that, I never again used my chutzpah – and I have tons – to bother professionals after hours.

Tolstoy was selectively deaf. When we met, the first five hundred pages of his book were stacked at my place. I could not see Tolstoy's face when I sat down. A good thing, too. I wanted to smack him.

Unable to focus on anything other than his writing, he asked me to "just read two pages." I agreed if he promised that after two, we could move on.

"A deal," Tolstoy said.

The two pages were about his great uncle, the only person who ever loved him, and two other relatives who did not. The writing was clunky and the self-pitying tone put me off.

"It's engaging. It has heart," I said. "Your descriptions are quite vivid."

In his profile, Tolstoy wrote that he liked to swim. I did, too. I moved the conversation to swimming.

Tolstoy could not get into the pool. He leafed through His Pages, more engaged in his manuscript than in me.

I asked about his college-age daughter whom he mentioned in his profile, then opened my wallet and pulled out a picture of Emily I had taken the previous year after she ran the New York City Marathon and showed it to him. "She's getting married."

He glanced at the photo. "Nice." That was it.

Not for me. I stared at the picture of my smiling daughter wearing her medal and holding the roses Teddy gave her. Twenty-five years earlier, I had pulled out a picture of her from my ski jacket on a chair lift in Aspen, during my last vacation with her father.

I was homesick in Aspen. I was homesick now. Homesick for a deep, human connection, for my home, for myself. Just three blocks from my apartment, why did I have to sit here? "My head is throbbing," I said, putting money for my share on the table. "I have to leave."

At home, I sprawled out on my living room sofa, relieved to be alone in my pale yellow space. Alone beat lonely with the wrong person. Alone beat lonely with a jerk.

Later I got off my sofa and opened my computer. A profile of a cute, sexy fifty-nine-year-old, twinkly-eyed man leaped out. His varied interests and closeness to his grown children got to me. His face got me more. He looked smart, cuddly, and as if he got the joke. I emailed him and received a witty, sweet response. After another round, I sent my phone number at his request. He didn't call.

I emailed asking why. He emailed that he had been traveling.

"Don't leave like that anymore," I wrote. *Why did I write and 'send' that? He'll think I'm a loon. A desperate loon. That's the end of him.*

"OK," he wrote back. *Phew.* Then he called.

Our conversation started with our hometowns, (Newton for him), then went to our children, work, and more. It was the Sunday afternoon of the Super Bowl. The Giants vs. the Patriots. That took a few minutes. As into the Super Bowl as always — not much — I had little to contribute. I was headed to a Super Bowl party but didn't want to go. He was on his way to one at a former Bostonian's. And did.

"We can do a post-game wrap up over dinner on Friday," he said.

"You do the wrap up. I'll eat."

He suggested we go to a restaurant in my neighborhood. We decided on Cornelia Street Café. "Should we meet there?" he asked.

"Or in my lobby." It just came out. I'd never given my address to a stranger before.

When I appeared, he was talking with my doorman and he didn't seem to want to stop. The spark that had been in his eyes in his photo was missing. So was he. Obviously, my looks disappointed him.

Walking down Sixth Avenue, he hardly spoke. I filled the space with questions. Creepy ones. About his health and the health of his parents, whether they had cancer or problems with their hearts, and if he ever had a colonoscopy. He hadn't. I had had a colonoscopy the week before and began describing the prep. Then, sounding like Annie Hall in the terrace scene, I stopped. "Forgive my taking a medical history. I'm nervous, not insane."

"I'm nervous, too," he said. "Unlike you, I become mute." He smiled. "And unlike you, I am insane."

We turned to each other. Finally.

"I'm sorry for grilling you," I said. "I thought I should fill up the space."

"It's refreshing." The twinkle in his eyes returned. "You're checking things out."

He checked me out at dinner, commenting on my energy and skin. We shared appetizers, entrees, and our personal histories.

"You're easy to talk to," he said, pushing up the sleeves of his black cashmere V-neck.

My heart did that little flutter thing. "And you have sexy arms."

I didn't want the evening to end. I did not want to part. I invited him to the top floor of Kimmel Hall, an NYU building right on Washington Square with spectacular views. Standing beside him taking in the scenery was perfect. Exciting and comfortable at the same time. He put his hand on my shoulder. Easy. Great.

On Saturday afternoon, I called Louise. "I had a date with someone new last night. I want to marry him."

A pause. Then, "Maybe wait to tell him," she said. "When's your next date?"

"I don't know. He didn't say anything about getting together again. What if he doesn't call?"

"I guess you won't be able to marry him."

He called an hour later. We had a second dinner the following week on February 13 at Five Points, a lovely East Village restaurant. The shirttails of his blue oxford cloth shirt hung out. He looked more rumpled and appealing than he had on Date One. Over brunch three days later, he mentioned he would have asked me out for Valentine's Day, but assumed some other guy, probably several, were after me.

Right! Take a number, get in line.

We added walks, daily calls, multi-daily calls, my missing him when he traveled on business, his missing me after two days, and swimming in his building's pool on our fourth date, displaying my less-than-perfect thighs.

I felt comfortable in his apartment right away. He had painted one living room wall coral and the long wall in his bedroom teal blue. Photos of his two grown children at various ages and lovely artwork hung all about. Books were everywhere.

Sitting on his sofa in my black Speedo with his gray tee shirt over it, snacking on mozzarella and sliced tomatoes that were on the cocktail table when I walked in, I thought of Wendy's parting words on moving day: "I'm making space for you to find someone great."

I turned to my Someone Great and it just came out, "Do you want to go with me to my daughter's wedding?" I told him the date, a year away, and that it was at Casa de Campo in the Dominican Republic. "Do you have plans that day?"

My invitation seemed to shock him more than the description of my colonoscopy prep had. He stared at me saying nothing for several seconds. "I'll check my calendar for next year when I get one," he said, smiling. At least it wasn't no.

I told Emily and Teddy when the three of us were out for a dinner a few nights later that I'd like to bring a date to their wedding and hoped it would be okay.

"That guy you met last week?" Emily said.

"Last month and yes."

"We don't know him. We've never met him, Mrs. K," said Teddy.

"You will. Soon.

He went on. "You haven't even mentioned him."

"She has, Teddy. This one's different. I can tell." Then to me, "What's his name, Mom?"

"Jonathan."

Five months into our relationship, I received an invitation to a friend's daughter's wedding, addressed to me. Not to me and "guest." I called the bride's mother to tell her I'd like to bring a date. She said the only people bringing guests had been living together at least six months or were engaged. "We'll be both soon," I said.

She bent her rule.

Sunday morning of the wedding, over breakfast at a diner, I asked Jonathan whether he had had a big or small wedding. He didn't respond immediately, then he asked, "Which time?"

"You were married more than once?"

He nodded. "The first was in college. For a few years. A starter marriage."

"You told me you were married once."

He looked away. "I thought you'd think less of me. Like I couldn't do it."

"So you lied."

"I was going to tell you. I wasn't sure how."

I got up. "I'm leaving."

"Do you still want me to go to the wedding later?" he asked.

I shrugged. He went to his apartment. I went to mine. I called my friend, Marsha, a psychotherapist who often counseled me between her forty-five minute hours, told her what had happened and asked for her advice.

"Do you share everything about yourself up front?"

"More or less."

"He probably thought you'd think he was a loser. He's still selling himself."

"But he lied."

"Yeah. Big deal."

"Maybe he's a big liar."

"I doubt it. He was embarrassed to tell you about wife number one." She went on, "You said Jonathan's fabulous and that you're ga ga about him. Until now, you picked jerks who gave you crumbs."

Crumbs. What I expected and thought I deserved for most of my life. If my mother could not love me, how could anyone?

"Let it go, Nancy."

I called Jonathan to tell him what time the ceremony started and to please not lie to me again. When he picked me up wearing a navy suit and adorable smile, I began to thaw. On the walk to the wedding in Chelsea, we barely spoke. Our silence was okay. Later, our first time cutting a rug, we moved together easily as if we had been partners for years. Being in his arms for the slow ones was more than okay. I knew where I belonged.

Jonathan's father died two months later at age ninety-four, walking from the kitchen after dinner, carrying his nightly scotch. He had not been sick.

Jonathan wanted me to come to Newton, but after the funeral. I took the train to Boston and paid a four-day *shiva* call.

"This must be hard for you," his brother-in-law said the first night.

Hard? At home beforehand, I had tried on all my serious clothes. Figuring out how to look right, support Jonathan, fit in and find my place when I clearly wasn't family, produced more than a bit of anxiety. My biggest worry: meeting his mom.

Friday evening six hours after the funeral, entering Jonathan's sister's and brother-in-law's, I spotted her immediately at the dining room table.

A Jewish Rose Kennedy was how Jonathan had described his ninety-year-old mother. Yes!

Her eyes were on me as I headed towards her, piercing me, studying me, taking me in. Did she notice the wrinkles on the black cotton dress I had been wearing all day and napped in on the train?

Bending down and taking her hand, I said, "I knew I'd be meeting you. I'm so sorry it has to be like this." I kissed her on the cheek. "I'm so sorry about your husband."

"I know you are," she shot back, a warmth coming through. I sensed she knew I meant business traveling all this way, and that her son might be serious about me. "Put your pocketbook down over there." She pointed to a chair in the corner of the dining room and to the open cartons of Chinese food on the sideboard. On what must have been one of the worst days of her life, she said, "The family ordered in dinner. Go make yourself a plate."

The following morning when Jonathan and I picked her up at her apartment to bring her back to his sister's, I asked her if she slept okay.

"Of course. Aren't you supposed to?"

The good news: our Jewish Rose spoke like that with everyone.

The better news: she and I lived in different states.

But apparently Jonathan and I lived on different planets. Whenever he introduced me I was "Nancy, a friend" or "Nancy, a dear friend."

On the third day of sitting *shiva*, I said, "This might not be the best time to bring it up, but I don't want to be your dear friend."

"What would you like to be?" Jonathan asked.

"I don't know." I did.

I wanted to commit until death do us part. I got an F with this ambiguity thing.

Mildred, long retired, had always driven home the

ambiguity thing. "You can't know the outcome," and "None of us know how it'll turn out," and "Life's too uncertain. Forget guarantees."

My current therapist, Alisa, whom I saw every few months for booster shots, put it a little differently. "Enjoy Jonathan's love and kindness now. Stay in the moment."

"That's like telling a heroin addict not to shoot up," I said. "What if he's only interested in something casual?"

"His behavior shows otherwise. But if he ultimately doesn't want what you do, then maybe you'll decide on a different path."

"I don't want a different path. I want Jonathan on mine."

She nodded. They all nodded.

Alisa liked reminding me that after my many years in therapy, she got "the cleaned up version" of me. "Whatever happens will happen," she said. "Meantime you're going to have to live with uncertainty."

I didn't want to live with uncertainty. I wanted to live with Jonathan.

Jonathan didn't just accompany me to Emily's and Teddy's wedding weekend in the Dominican Republic. He listened to me practice my rehearsal dinner toast, made our plane reservations, and paid for the tickets. From the moment we arrived at the seaside resort with its long, palm-lined entrance, we shared the beauty. The calm, blue Caribbean beckoned. Following the bride and groom's poolside welcome party, we went right down to the beach and dove in.

Jonathan's presence made the most important occasion of my life more fun. But it did not alleviate my nervousness about seeing my ex-husband. Talk about things turning out different from expectations.

When will I ever learn?

Don did the initial reaching out. He approached me and hugged me, and we talked with each other and then as a foursome, with his long-time partner, Lynne, and with Jonathan.

At the rehearsal dinner on the beach at dusk, two sentences into my speech, I looked out at the water, the stars, the happy faces, mostly the bride's and groom's, and the butterflies in my stomach quieted down. When I finished, Don came over to me – the first person to do so – and told me it was great.

The next night at the wedding dinner at Altos de Chavon, a re-creation of a Mediterranean style European village overlooking the Chavon River, Don gave his toast and then stopped at my table on the way back to his and asked me how he did.

"Wonderful!" I said, touched.

During the father/bride dance, walking over to Lynne seemed like the most natural thing to do. "I always wondered how I'd feel at this moment," I said to her. "It's choking me up more than I expected."

"They both look so young," she said. A pause, then "Jonathan seems nice."

"He is."

When the band played a fast song, I asked Don to dance. "Jonathan's a good guy," he said.

"Thank you. You found your right person too."

"It's thirty years now," he said. "It's not like we're new."

"So I'm a little late saying it. Some things take a while."

A student's essay about her dog, Tucker, came to mind. When Tucker died, the family buried him in a New Jersey pet cemetery called Paws and Peace. She visited Tucker's grave every week for months. When she decided she wanted another dog and found one she liked, before she could give the new pet a home, she went to the cemetery for Tucker's blessings. Of course!

Three months after the wedding, Jonathan and I made a Seder. Our children met and were comfortable together. We did a Cliffs Notes version of the Haggadah. Each child asked one the four questions. The following day, I asked Jonathan one. "Those women you went with," I said, referring to the two girlfriends he had had since his divorce. "Did you not want to marry *them* or did you not want to get *married*?"

"Them."

"*Them*" was all he said that night.

A few weeks later at Five Points where we had gone on our second date, Jonathan got down on one knee and proposed. I had a hunch this might happen. I'd been asking on a daily basis if and when he'd propose.

I said yes. Of course I said yes. I hugged him hard, not

wanting to let go.

"I hope you didn't propose because of my subtle hinting," I said.

"I had the idea myself," he said. "I would have asked you much sooner if you hadn't nudged."

The next morning I called Emily. "Jonathan asked me to marry him."

"And . . ."

"I said yes."

We cried.

Our wedding took place six months later on a Saturday evening before forty close relatives and friends at a beautiful party loft on Fifth Avenue. The day of the wedding, Jonathan put photos of our parents and families all around the loft. The ceremony began with our three children and Teddy carrying in a *chuppah*. Our guests filled their plates and spirits. Everybody danced. Most of the night, I was in my husband's arms. I only got to the shrimp.

We honeymooned in St. Lucia at Jade Mountain. Our room, high on a hill, had three walls, with the opening facing the Pitons, two dramatic volcanic spires.

Van service existed between the high rooms and the beach, but we chose to take the four hundred and twenty-three steps down each morning and back up to our three-walled sanctuary each afternoon. On our way up one afternoon, a New York couple we met on the beach joined us. I walked with the woman. Jonathan and her husband followed. Twelve years younger than we were, she told me they were celebrating their twenty-fifth anniversary a year early. They both had terminal cancer.

When we left them, Jonathan said he and her husband talked about their work, previous vacations, and our Jade Mountain rooms. Theirs had a pool. Ours did not. "Lucky them," Jonathan said.

"Didn't the husband tell you how sick they were?"

Not a word. We saw them again at the end of the vacation at the St. Lucia airport in the customs line. She and I went to the ladies room together. She told me they were both very depressed about going home to resume treatments at Sloan Kettering.

On the plane, Jonathan told me that the husband still did not say a word about their cancers. "Men and women are so different about what they discuss and don't, aren't they?" he said.

I nodded. Life was so fragile. And often so sweet. I reached for my husband's hand.

I was sixty when I met Jonathan. He was fifty-nine. Finding love at our age – at any age – is grand. The couple we met was a reminder of how quickly it slips away.

"Let's go to Paris for your sixty-fifth birthday," Jonathan said one night. When the Hebrew calligrapher offered to take me to Paris for my fortieth birthday, I stared at him. Nothing came out of my mouth. Paris was for lovers.

I reached over and kissed my husband. "Yes, let's."

Jonathan did a great job arranging our vacations. I did a better job coming with. Yet as the months passed,

I did not really want to travel or think of going or being elsewhere as much as he did. I took daily trips at home in my writing. I loved my routine.

Constant togetherness threw me. And not because he squeezed the toothpaste in the middle or left his socks on the rug. I did not know how to have both intimacy and space.

How did people juggle the two? Now part of a couple, I seemed to be losing myself.

Another thing I struggled with: responding when he said something that upset me. I did what I'd done in the past: jabbed back, got upset, stormed around, and stormed out. We both knew how to jab. Like guilt and angst, sarcasm was in our blood.

One Sunday I had enough. Enough companionship. Enough tit for tat. I went to the college library where I teach and I wrote, staying until closing time. Then I walked home.

From the street, I noticed our second-floor apartment was dark. A pit formed in my stomach. Where was my sweetheart? Had he had enough of me? Was he sick? How come he wasn't home?

When I unlocked the front door, I heard him in the master bathroom. He was under the sink with his shirt off, sweating. He had a wrench in his hand.

Jonathan was quite a handyman.

"Hey, honey," he said, his eyes lighting up.

The pit in my stomach disappeared. No matter what transpired earlier or how we'd been getting along, Jonathan's eyes lit up when he saw me. So did mine with him.

"Anything more you want to discuss?" Jonathan asked.

I pointed to the sink. "Did you really fix the drip?"

"I really did."

"That means I have to stop saying there's a little drip in the bathroom."

"Call me something else," he said.

In the alcove was a carton of books he had brought down from his apartment. We had no space for them until the week before when he put up new shelves. "Should we keep our books separate or should they mingle?" I asked him now.

"They should mingle," he said.

We started to put books on the new shelves. Then I stopped. "Okay if we do this tomorrow?"

"Sure."

I put on classic Sinatra and we danced to a couple of slow ones.

We continue to learn how to express our discomfort in the moment. Easy? No. But who said it would all be easy?

Finding love, for me, has been a challenge. Having space and intimacy is ongoing work. In my sixties, I continue to work at it.

Neither Jonathan nor I had been to the Southwest. With a lightweight computer he bought for me; a lightweight camera I bought for him; the three things Uncle Lou, the director of Camp Tamakwa used to put on the "What to Bring" list under the heading "Yourself" – a sense of humor, a desire to learn, and a willingness to share; along with our willingness to give each other space – we took a fifteen-day road trip through Colorado, Arizona, Utah, and New Mexico.

At Bryce Canyon, Utah, after a scary, steep hike to the bottom and a scarier climb back up, we walked along the rim making snowballs, awed by the shapes and colors of the terrain.

The most arresting formations were the hoodoos – tall, thin brown/pink spires of rock like totem poles with tops that widened out. The name "hoodoo" cracked us up. Each time we saw one, we said the word aloud.

Sharing the beauty with Jonathan came second only to sharing a laugh.

From Bryce, we went to Zion National Park. On our first full day, after a long morning hike with the sun beating down, we were eager to swim. The pool, big and inviting, was fairly empty.

Jonathan dove in at the deep end and began his laps. I walked slowly down the steps at the shallow end, splashing my face, arms and neck. By the time I got in, he was ready for a break in the Jacuzzi where he joined four other guests.

I planned to swim a half an hour, as I do at the gym at home, but in the middle of my second lap, I noticed a brownish object at the bottom near the shallow end. It was the size and shape of a banana. I looked around. No one else was swimming. A woman in the shallow end was splashing water on her face. A little girl, holding onto the ladder at the deep end, practiced her flutter kick. I did two more laps of the breast stroke without putting my head in the water. The brown object was still there. I got out and into the Jacuzzi beside my husband.

"That was quick," he said.

"Something's in the pool," I announced.

Two people, in the middle of a conversation, stopped and glanced our way. The two others, holding beer cans, talked too loud to hear.

Moving closer to Jonathan, I whispered, "A brown something. Please could you go see what it is? It looks like . . ."

Jonathan helped, "A hoodoody."

I nodded.

Fortunately, no one in the Jacuzzi cared what I saw in the pool, or what we had to say. The beer people continued drinking. The conversers continued to converse.

I went on. "Please, Jonathan, could you go find maintenance?"

Jonathan walked up the four steps of the Jacuzzi, over to the pool, and looked in. Unable to see anything, he turned to me, shrugging, and then disappeared into the men's room, emerging moments later carrying a bunch of paper towels and wearing a white cloth towel around his head, the way he did on our honeymoon in St. Lucia at the beach in the heat of the day. Talk about arresting. My sweet, dark, sexy husband bent down to get whatever was at the bottom of the pool, wrapped it in the paper towels and brought it to the Jacuzzi.

"Look!" Inside the wet towels were several brown leaves. "They must have fallen last night." He pointed to the enormous tree next to the pool. The night before it had poured.

"Thank goodness it wasn't a doody or a hoodoody," I said.

Jonathan smiled. "I didn't think it was."

Of course not. My easy-going husband thinks most things are no big deals. I make hoodoodies out of brown leaves.

I am learning. I have so much to learn. Admittedly, shit happens. In most of life and in most swimming pools, it does not.

"How come you're wearing a towel on your head?" I asked.

Jonathan shrugged. "In case I picked up a piece of you-know-what, I didn't want anyone to recognize me carrying it."

That night, we ordered fish tacos and margaritas. My husband raised his glass. "If you didn't get that I was madly in love with you before I picked up what might have been shit, I hope you do now."

I nodded.

After dinner, we took the shuttle bus through Zion Park for a two-hour information tour with the ranger. It was an illuminating talk, but it did not engage me as much as a young couple with an adorable little girl sitting across the aisle. The girl, around six, all dressed up in a light blue dress and white Mary Janes and holding a little white pocketbook by the strap, sat on her mother's lap at the window seat, listening to the ranger and staring out the window. Every so often, she asked her parents, in a quiet voice, a question about what she was looking at and what the ranger was saying. They took turns answering, in whispers. The mother stroked her hair.

As it grew dark, the girl put her head down on her mother's lap, her feet up on her father's, and her thumb in her mouth, making loud sucking noises as she drifted off to sleep.

A summer Saturday from my childhood came to mind. My sister was at overnight camp. It was just my parents and me. My mother decided we would have dinner on the Canadian side of Niagara Falls. I clapped my hands.

"Let's go to the top of the General Brock Hotel," I said. We had eaten there on special occasions. It had a spectacular view of the Horseshoe Falls.

"It's for tourists. The food's not great," Dad said. "We know better restaurants."

"I'm not going to your better restaurants," I said.

My parents, looking at each other, smiled. Dad went on. "We don't have a sitter."

"I'll treat."

I got my little red plastic pocketbook and put in all the money I had in the world. Twenty dollars: my birthday and Chanukah presents from my grandmothers. At Niagara Falls, my parents mentioned the names of two other restaurants with good food. I reminded them I'd pay.

As we got off the elevator on the top floor of the General Brock, we could see the falls lit up in pink and green and yellow. The maitre d' led us to a table in the center of the fancy dining room. The window tables were occupied. Several times throughout the meal, I got up, walked to the window, and looked out. When we finished eating, the waiter put the bill in front of my father. He picked it up.

"Coming here was my idea," I said. "I told you I'd treat."

My mother and father both had twinkles in their eyes.

"She did, Max. Why don't you let Nancy pay?" My mother sounded nice, like she was proud of me, like I was her big girl.

My father handed me the bill. Drinks and dinner came to sixteen dollars and change. I unzipped my red plastic pocketbook, took out what I had, and counted it. No one spoke as I put my money on the table.

Riding home in our silver blue Chevy convertible with the top down, I sat between them, feeling proud I delivered what I said I would. Despite a tiny fear about my empty piggy bank, I knew my father would come through with my weekly allowance and if no one gave my grandmothers the stupid idea I'd like a sweater for my birthday, they'd continue to come through with the gelt.

My mother taught me to pay for what I wanted.

I did. And I have. Whenever she saw me upset or depressed or impatient, she made sure to share another important truth: good things take a long time to develop. Her lessons, along with my father's two biggies have become my tickets to every day.

It only takes one, Dad would say when an editor rejected my work or I had another miserable date. And the other, for the ages, for us all: we take ourselves with us wherever we go.

That summer night after I paid for our dinner at Niagara Falls, as we crossed the Peace Bridge from Canada to Buffalo, the breeze cooling my face and my hair, with Mom and Dad, my first and best teachers on either side of me, I felt protected. Safe. And very loved.

It didn't get better than that.

Until now.

◆

Acknowledgments

I have been blessed with the wisdom, inspiration, intelligence, kindness, patience, humor and support of many people long before I began writing *Finding Mr. Rightstein*. I am grateful to the following for their contributions directly, unwittingly, and posthumously to this book and to my life:

Judith Appelbaum, Barbara Barak, the Birnbaums (Margie, Buzz, Kristen, Jeff), Inez Canvasser, Alan Carrel, Deborah Chasman, Laura Cronk, Elizabeth Crow, Jill Dell'Abate, Allan Fallow, Carol Feind, Marjorie Frank, Lewis Frumkes, Julie Gaines, Judy Garfield, Ellen Goldstein Jim Howe, Leah Iannone, Hayes Jacobs, Luis Jaramillo, Judy Judelson, Elaine Kessel, Cindy Kurtin, Elinor Lipman, Lorrie Lynch, Doreen Margolin, Phil Margolin, Michael Nach, Peggy Schwartz, Bill Schwartz, Justin Sherwood, Susan Silverman, Stephanie von Hirschberg, Yael Yisrael, Doris Zich, Matthew Zich, and Rebecca Zich.

– Thank you to my Buffalo relatives, friends, classmates, and everyone who charcoal broiled my hot dogs at Ted's.

– Thank you to my dates for providing a wellspring of material.

– Thank you to my therapists who for different reasons will also remain nameless.

– Thank you to my internist, Dr. Charles Silvera, for prescribing JDate, not meds and to my gynecologist, Dr. Jill Fishbane-Mayer, for doing the same thing. And they don't even know each other.

– Thank you to my students for allowing me to try to teach them the things I am supposed to know.

– Thank you to those I did not mention because of my negligence, memory lapses, or because they don't want to be associated with me.

My most heartfelt thanks to my most Rightstein people:

– my smart, caring editors Mary Azrael and Kendra Kopelke and Pantea A. Tofangchi, Christine Drawl, and Saralyn Lyons of Passager Books for working so hard to make this book more wonderful than I imagined.

– my parents, Max and Esther Davidoff, now sharing early bird dinners in heaven. Their love, humor, lessons, spirits and souls are with me wherever I go.

– my daughter and son-in-law, Emily Kelton Owens and Ted Owens, and their precious children, Ryan and Charlotte, who occupy the core of my heart and fill me up more than words can say.

– my husband, Jonathan Zich, my true love and my ticket to every day.

Portions of "In the Beginning" appeared in the same or different form in *The New York Times Sunday Magazine, The Buffalo News,* and *Welter Literary Journal.*

A portion of "Moving Along" appeared in a different form in *The New York Times.*

A portion of "After the Early Bird Dinners" appeared in a different form in the *Minetta Review.*

A portion of "When One Door Closes . . . Another Door Shuts" appeared in *Passager Journal.*

Also from Passager Books

A Cartography of Peace
Jean L. Connor

Improvise in the Amen Corner
Larnell Custis Butler

A Little Breast Music
Shirley J. Brewer

A Hinge of Joy
Jean L. Connor

Everything Is True at Once
Bart Galle

Perris, California
Norma Chapman

Nightbook
Steve Matanle

I Shall Go As I Came
Ellen Kirvin Dudis

Keeping Time:
150 Years of Journal Writing
edited by Mary Azrael & Kendra Kopelke

Burning Bright:
Passager Celebrates 21 Years
edited by Mary Azrael & Kendra Kopelke

Hot Flash Sonnets
Moira Egan

Beyond Lowu Bridge
Roy Cheng Tsung

Because There Is No Return
Diana Anhalt

Never the Loss of Wings
Maryhelen Snyder

The Want Fire
Jennifer Wallace

Little Miracles
James K. Zimmerman

View from the Hilltop
A Collection by The North Oaks Writers
edited by Barbara Sherr Roswell and Christine Drawl

The Chugalug King & Other Stories
Andrew Brown

Gathering the Soft
Becky Dennison Sakellariou
Paintings by Tandy Zorba

In legends, the crane stands for longevity, peace, harmony, good fortune and fidelity. A high flyer, it is cherished for its ability to see both heaven and earth. These ancient, magnificent birds, so crucial in the wild as an "umbrella species," are now endangered and must be protected.

Passager Books is dedicated to making public the passions of a generation vital to our survival.

Finding Mr. Rightstein was designed and typeset using Adobe InDesign. The pages are set in Adobe Garamond Pro and Futura.
Cover art and design by Pantea Amin Tofangchi.

Printed in 2016 by Spencer Printing, Honesdale, PA.